Excavations of the royal palace at Ugarit (P. C. Craigie)

UGARIT
AND THE
OLD TESTAMENT

by

PETER C. CRAIGIE

Grand Rapids
WILLIAM B. EERDMANS PUBLISHING COMPANY

Copyright © 1983 by Wm. B. Eerdmans Publishing Company
255 Jefferson Ave. S.E., Grand Rapids, Mich. 49503
All rights reserved
Printed in the United States of America

Library of Congress Cataloging in Publication Data

Craigie, Peter C.
Ugarit and the Old Testament.

Bibliography: p. 103
1. Ugarit (Ancient city) 2. Bible. O.T. — Criticism
criticism, interpretation, etc. 3. Ugaritic literature — Relation to the Old Testament. 4. Mythology,
Semitic. I. Title.
DS99.U35C7 1983   939'.4   82-16448
ISBN 0-8028-1928-1 (pbk.)

CONTENTS

LIST OF MAPS AND FIGURES

PREFACE

IT is almost impossible, nowadays, to read a detailed book or commentary on the Old Testament that does not contain some reference to Ugarit. And yet for many readers, little is known of the ancient civilization of Ugarit beyond the fact that its data are somehow relevant to the study of the Old Testament. The present book is an introduction to Ugarit, the city, its language and literature, and the relevance of the whole to Old Testament studies. It is written for those who have an interest in the biblical world and the environment in which the Old Testament was born.

Many friends and colleagues have been of assistance in the preparation of this book. I should like particularly to express my thanks to Gabriel Saadé of Latakia, Syria, for his hospitality and help during a visit to Ras Shamra. And Dr. J.-L. Cunchillos, in Paris, was of enormous assistance in guiding me to the libraries of that great city.

UGARIT
AND THE
OLD TESTAMENT

Chapter I:
NEW LIGHT ON
THE BIBLICAL WORLD

THE Bible is not, in principle, a difficult document to read. Its message and substance are clear, and from the beginning it was written for the ordinary person. But the modern reader faces a problem unknown to the original readers and hearers of the biblical message: the passage of time has imposed the gulf of centuries between the modern reader and the text. And that gulf in turn is wide, for the modern world has changed radically from that in which the biblical narrative is set. Hence, it is difficult for a citizen of the twentieth century simply to sit down and read all of the Bible with understanding. Although the problem exists potentially for the entire Bible, it is particularly acute in the case of the Old Testament, set as it is in an historical past between 2½ and 3½ millennia ago.

For the majority of modern readers, the problem created by the passage of time is aggravated still further by other difficulties, specifically those of language and culture. We may speak any one of several modern languages, but Classical Hebrew and Aramaic are not normally languages familiar to us. And our culture, though profoundly shaped and influenced by the biblical tradition, sets us still further apart from the culture of the biblical world. If, through some warp in time, the figures of the biblical world could enter temporarily into our modern world, they would be totally lost, and the reverse would be no less true; if we were present briefly in the biblical world, we would not be attuned to its norms and patterns of activity.

Thus every modern reader of the Bible, and especially of the Old Testament, faces a problem, that of bridging the gaps that separate the ancient world from the modern. If no attempt is made to bridge those gaps, then the lack of familiarity with biblical language and culture will contribute to a failure to understand the

3

biblical message. For though the biblical message is eternal, its form and setting are historical and temporal. And though the biblical message is not complex, we are for the most part so profoundly unfamiliar with the form in which it is set, that we can easily miss its simplicity and power.

Initially, the recognition of this dilemma facing the modern reader of the Bible may be disturbing. It is as though our births in the twentieth century have been a disadvantage to us, and indeed as though those yet to be born will be still further disadvantaged, separated in time even more than the current generation from the period of the biblical world. But when once we have recognized our distance from the biblical world, we may also begin to see appropriate remedies for the problem.

It is true of reading in general that the capacity to understand is influenced enormously by what the reader already knows. Thus, if one were to visit a library and withdraw two very different books, both in the English language, the ability to read them with comprehension would be profoundly affected by background knowledge and general education. Let us say that one of the two books was a work of fiction, John MacDonald's *Condominium*; even if Florida had never been visited and the ownership of a condominium were a distant dream (or nightmare), nevertheless the average North American would be well equipped to read MacDonald's novel with comprehension. But if the other book drawn from the library were entitled *The Way of Lao Tzu*, translated from Chinese into excellent English, the average North American would find it exceptionally difficult to read with understanding. For without some prior knowledge of the history and thought of China more than two thousand years in the past, *The Way of Lao Tzu*, though not intrinsically difficult, would be very heavy reading. We are commonly deceived into thinking that the reading of the Old Testament is like reading modern fiction; in other words, we think that we already have in our heads the knowledge that would equip us to read with understanding, simply because the biblical language itself (in translation) has become so familiar to us in the Western world. But in reality, when we approach the Old Testament, we are doing something akin to turning to the Old Chinese classic; for though *The Way of Lao Tzu* and the Old Testament are very different in substance, they both come to us from an ancient and foreign world.

The problem, in other words, does not lie primarily in the Old Testament but in ourselves, in the lack of general knowledge of the biblical world that would enable us to open its pages and read with understanding. The only way to remedy the deficiency within ourselves is to build up a store of knowledge in order to equip ourselves better to understand the words that we read. But how is that to be done, for the Old Testament comes to us from a world long past and dead? Though there are several ways in which that question can be addressed, one of the key answers to the question in the twentieth century is to be found in the results of modern archaeology.

During the last two centuries, we have seen the birth of a new discipline, commonly called "biblical archaeology," which may enable us to get back to the biblical world in a way scarcely possible in the preceding centuries. Beginning in a systematic fashion in the nineteenth century, and burgeoning in the twentieth century, the archaeological exploration of the biblical lands has put a mass of data at the modern reader's disposal. The spade, the trowel, and the delicate sweeping of the archaeologist's brush have pushed back the soils of time to reveal remains: buildings, objects, and written texts. And the discoveries themselves have provided the raw material from which to reconstruct the details of life and thought in biblical times. When we absorb the data provided by archaeological research, we are filling the gaps in our knowledge; we are equipping ourselves to read the ancient text with understanding by reducing the gap between our own century and the biblical centuries.

And yet, in the latter half of the twentieth century, there has been an extraordinary reversal. Whereas a century and a half ago the discipline of modern archaeology was still in its infancy, now it has grown beyond all bounds. In theory this massive growth is good, providing extensive knowledge of the biblical world; in practice it is formidable, for even the specialists cannot keep up to date with the massive amount of information that is constantly being recovered. In biblical archaeology, as in so many other areas of modern thought, we are experiencing the trauma of "information explosion."

One of the consequences of this information explosion is that the results of the new knowledge are being filtered into popular books about the Bible, yet the general reader is not normally aware of the source and background of the information. It is scarcely possible to read a modern commentary on the Old Testament without coming across frequent references to such names as Qumran and Ugarit. Qumran, the place where the famous Dead Sea Scrolls were found, is now reasonably well known; Ugarit, though at least as important as Qumran, is less well known. Yet the word Ugarit is not only frequently used in modern books about the Bible, but is also an area of discovery which has changed and contributed immensely to the translation of the Bible and its interpretation.

And so this short book is about the ancient city of Ugarit or Ras Shamra, as it is called nowadays in Arabic. From one perspective, it could be argued that Ugarit was merely one city among many in the biblical world. If such were the case, it would still be a subject worth knowing. But Ugarit is more significant than that; its archives and ancient texts have added fundamentally to our knowledge of the Old Testament world, to an extent far greater than has been the case with other archaeological sites excavated in the world east of the Mediterranean. Hence, this book is intended to be a guide for the general reader of the Old Testament. It will fill in some of the story lying behind the use of the word Ugarit that is so common in modern textbooks and commentaries. And it is hoped that it will contribute also towards bridging the gap between the modern world and the ancient world, so that the contemporary reader of the Old Testament can turn to that ancient book with more profit.

Chapter II:
THE REDISCOVERY
OF A LOST CITY

In the spring of 1928, a farm worker was ploughing some land on the Mediterranean coast of Syria; his name was Mahmoud Mella az-Zir and he lived close to a bay called Minet el-Beida. The tip of his plough ran into stone just beneath the surface of the soil; when he examined the obstruction, he found a large man-made flagstone. He cleared away the earth, raised the stone, and beneath it he saw a short subterranean passageway leading into an ancient tomb. Entering the tomb, he discovered a number of ancient objects of potential value; these he sold to a dealer in antiquities. Though he could not have known it at the time, the agricultural worker had opened up more than a tomb on that spring day; he had opened a door which was to lead to extraordinary discoveries concerning ancient history and civilization, and even to a new appraisal of the nature and contents of the Old Testament.

The agricultural worker did not initially publicize his discovery, but inevitably news of the find leaked out. The discovery had been made in the state of the Alaouites (Alawiya); now a part of modern Syria, at that time it was a territory which had been formed by the Supreme Council of Allies after World War I and was under French mandate. Word of the discovery came to the French governor of the territory, M. Schoeffler, being conveyed to him both in a police report and in a communication from M. Bruno Michel, a businessman in Latakia, the territorial capital. Schoeffler, on receiving the information, notified the director of the Antiquities Service of Syria and Lebanon, Charles Virolleaud.

Virolleaud had been director of antiquities for the region since October 1, 1920, and he was well acquainted with his territory. He knew enough about the location of the find to decide that the matter was worthy of further investigation. He sent an assistant,

7

Léon Albanèse, on a short trip to examine the place where the tomb had been discovered. Albanèse set out for the site of the discovery in the latter part of March 1928. In many ways his brief report was not very encouraging. He provided a description of a tell (mound) called Ras Shamra, a few hundred meters inland from the coast; he added a terse description of the tomb found by the agricultural laborer, and an equally short description of one or two objects which were recovered, probably Cypriote in character.

If the future of the investigations had depended entirely on Albanèse's report, it is likely that the story might finish at this point, but there were a number of reasons which prompted further investigation. There was, first, the nature of the place where the initial discovery had been made. Minet el-Beida means "White Harbor" in Arabic; although the bay was not functioning as a harbor in 1928 (only a few local men used it for their fishing boats), it was a natural port. Minet el-Beida was a bay, its mouth guarded by the white limestone rocks which gave it its name. In 1927, René Dussaud (curator of oriental antiquities in the Louvre) had suggested in a book that this bay could be the ancient harbor referred to in Greek texts as *Leukos Limen* ("White Harbor"). In other words, its desolate situation in 1928 might hide the possibility that in ancient times Minet el-Beida may have been a thriving seaport.

But there were other reasons for further investigation, among them the legend and stories which survived among the residents of that area. One tradition had it that in ancient times there had been a glorious city, rich in silver and gold, which was so large that several days were required to make a circuit of its walls. The stories had developed, no doubt, to account for discoveries of gold and other precious objects which had been made from time to time. And in 1928 there were still some local residents who could recall, painfully, the treasure-hunting excavations undertaken at the command of Turkish authorities in the late nineteenth century. All this evidence pointed to something worthy of further exploration.

During the winter months of 1928-1929, preparations began in order to send a proper archaeological team to Minet el-Beida in the spring of 1929. Claude F.A. Schaeffer was chosen as leader of the team; he was, at that time, thirty years old and employed

FIGURE 1: Latakia, Ras Shamra, and Minet el-Beida

in the archaeological museum in Strasbourg, France. His second-in-command was another French archaeologist, Georges Chenet; there were four other members of the team: Jean de Jaegher, Roger Vissuzaine, Paul Pironin, and Jacques Fagard. Their excavation was to be under the patronage of the Académie des Inscriptions et Belles Lettres of Paris; it also received support from the French Ministry of Education, the Louvre, and the local

9

government in Latakia, which was only about seven miles to the south of Minet el-Beida.

Schaeffer and his team arrived in Latakia towards the end of March 1929 and made preparations for the short (but difficult) journey from there to the exploration site. At first he thought it would be possible to make the trip by car, but he was forced to turn back, "despite the staunchness of my American-made cars," as he wrote later. He arranged a small caravan, with seven camels to carry his supplies, and finally set out for Minet el-Beida on Saturday, March 30, 1929, accompanied by some Syrian horsemen for protection. Before leaving, he arranged with General de Bigault du Granrut for a small detachment of twenty soldiers to be assigned to him for protection against brigands who roamed the area, making it dangerous for unprotected parties.

The caravan party left Schaeffer and his team with their supplies at Minet el-Beida and returned to Latakia, but the following morning the promised detachment of twenty soldiers arrived. By that Monday preparations were complete, and early on Tuesday morning, April 2, Schaeffer began his excavations. Many of the soldiers exchanged their rifles for picks, and only a few retained their weapons and maintained guard. Soon, the initial work force of soldiers was expanded by the arrival of local Alaouites, who were initially suspicious, but were willing enough to work when they perceived that they would receive a fair wage.

After only three days of excavating at Minet el-Beida at the southeast corner of the bay, it was clear to Schaeffer that he had discovered the necropolis (cemetery) of an ancient city. Objects were discovered almost immediately, being recovered at depths between two to six feet. Within a few days, Schaeffer and his team had discovered a complete ceramic table serivce, considerably more than three thousand years old. But objects more extraordinary than ancient ceramics were discovered; a statuette of the Canaanite god Resheph was found, partially adorned with gold and silver plating (which can now be seen in the Louvre), together with a beautiful nude figure of the goddess Astarte holding flowers in her hand. These two discoveries prompted Schaeffer to send a rider off to Latakia with a message to be sent by radio to Paris: "The treasure of Minet el-Beida is found!"

The initial explorations of the necropolis were undertaken fairly close to the coast; later, Schaeffer moved to the southern quarter of the necropolis and began to dig there. Again he met with success; three more tombs were found, apparently the royal tombs of long-dead kings. The tombs had already been penetrated by plunderers, probably centuries in the past, so they contained no enormous treasure; the plunderers, however, had worked in haste and had left a number of objects behind, including gold rings and an exquisite ivory box, which at one time had contained the jewels of a queen.

The first five weeks of excavation in the necropolis area had been met with such remarkable success that it would have been easy for the excavators to continue digging in the same area for the remainder of the season. In fact, they changed the location of their excavations after a little more than five weeks, to follow up a suggestion. Only a week after Schaeffer's team had started their work, they were visited on the site by René Dussaud, on April 9-10. Dussaud was a scholar of considerable distinction; as curator of oriental antiquities at the Louvre he had been influential in persuading l'Académie des Inscriptions et Belles Lettres to support the expedition to Syria. He suggested to Schaeffer that it would be worthwhile exploring the large tell, Ras Shamra, to the east of the necropolis. The recovered city of the dead must have been

FIGURE 2: Early excavations: Minet el-Beida and Ras Shamra

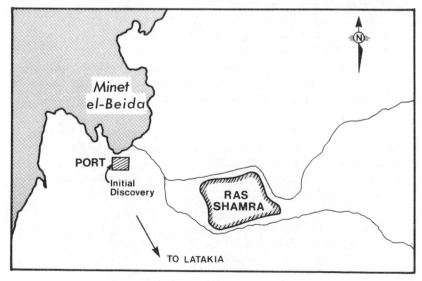

close to a city of the living; perhaps the large mound hid the remains of the once-living city.

On Thursday, May 9, Schaeffer transferred his efforts to the tell. Ras Shamra ("Fennel Head"), named after the aromatic plants that grew so profusely on its slopes, was a large mound, a little more than sixty feet high and covering an area of approximately fifty acres. The tell was flanked on both sides, north and south, by two streams which join just west of the tell before flowing into the ocean at Minet el-Beida. The size of the tell presented Schaeffer with a problem; given the strong possibility that the ruins of an ancient city lay beneath the surface, in which section of the large area should he begin to dig? If he chose the wrong place, he might find nothing, or at least nothing of importance. More by good judgment than good luck, he determined to start at the highest point of the tell, its northeast quarter; in that section, he noticed what might be the remains of walls, partially covered by the undergrowth, which he thought might mark the location of an ancient palace. But there was another reason that helped to determine the starting point of his excavations on the tell. Local rumor had it that tiny cylinders and golden objects had been found in the orchard of olive trees that lay at the foot of the northeastern slope of the tell. If the rumor had any validity, Schaeffer speculated that rain water might have washed the objects from the surface of the tell to the orchard below. So he began to dig.

Once again, Schaeffer's team met with immediate success. As the ground was cleared, there were revealed the foundations of a large and ancient structure which had been destroyed long ago by fire. A number of objects were retrieved from the ruins: a bronze dagger, an Egyptian torso carved from granite and bearing Egyptian hieroglyphic writing, and a sandstone stele (monument) dedicated to the Canaanite god, Baal Ṣapuna. Then Schaeffer moved again, this time about twenty-five yards to the east. There he excavated the room of a building, which was later identified as a school or library; the room was divided by three pillars. It was at this spot, on May 14, 1929, that the first clay tablet, bearing cuneiform writing on its surface, was found.

The discovery of a clay tablet containing writing was not in itself surprising. Many ancient libraries, especially from ancient Mesopotamia (modern Iraq), had been discovered during the nineteenth and early twentieth centuries; those discoveries had

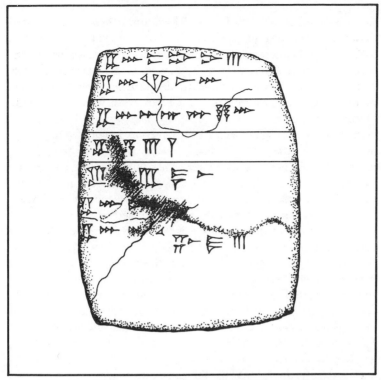

FIGURE 3: The reverse of a clay tablet discovered at Ras Shamra, 1929, listing names of persons

made it clear that in Mesopotamian (Babylonian and Assyrian) civilization, clay was the basic material used for writing purposes, the equivalent of modern paper. While the clay was soft, wedge-shaped marks were imprinted with a stylus; this is the meaning of cuneiform writing. Then the soft marked clay was baked hard so that the writing was permanently imprinted on its surface.

Thus the discovery of a tablet containing cuneiform writing was gratifying, but not initially startling. In the days that followed, more clay tablets were found in the ruins, some of them still in the piles in which they were stacked when the building had been destroyed. The extraordinary nature of the discovery came only when the cuneiform writing was examined in more detail; it was not the cuneiform known from ancient Mesopotamian tablets, an exceedingly complex system involving the use of several hundred symbols. Most of these tablets unearthed on the mound of Ras Shamra were in a previously unknown type of cuneiform; there were only a few symbols, approximately twenty-six or twenty-seven as it then appeared. In other words, it looked as if these tablets from Ras Shamra, apparently dating from more than twelve hundred years before the time of Christ, were written in a kind of cuneiform alphabet.

Schaeffer once again sent a messenger to Latakia. The governor, M. Schoeffler, accompanied by his director of finance, arrived at Ras Shamra two days later. They witnessed the uncovering of more clay tablets and so were able to attest their absolute authenticity. Meanwhile, a message was sent by radio to the Academy in Paris, and the team began to receive their first congratulatory messages. It is not often that a lost language is rescued from the refuse of an ancient mound!

The excavation team still had not finished their season of digging. A trench was dug, adjacent to the place where the tablets were found, and in that trench they discovered a cache of seventy-four weapons and tools. Among the tools were five axe heads bearing inscriptions in the alphabetic cuneiform identified earlier. Later to be important in deciphering the writing system, they now are displayed in the Louvre.

Eventually, in mid-May, the first excavation came to a halt.

FIGURE 4: **Axe head from Ras Shamra, with cuneiform inscription**

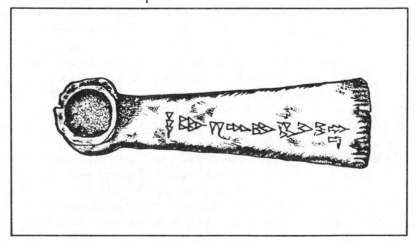

As the summer months approached, the increasing heat made digging impossible. Even before the end of the season, the excavators had been working from 4 a.m. until 10 a.m. and then taking a break in the heat of the day; work would resume about 3 p.m. and continue until nightfall. The temperature, together with the increase of violent activity by bandits in the neighborhood, brought the first mission to a close. (News had been received of the murder of a French archaeologist not too far from Ras Shamra; he had been killed while resisting robbers.) Schaeffer sealed the shafts which had been opened and established a guardpost on Ras Shamra so that the site could be guarded in the summer and winter months ahead.

Then Schaeffer faced the problem of transporting the articles which had been found back to Latakia. He ruled out road travel as too rough for his precious cargo; he hired a boat onto which the articles were loaded in the ancient White Harbor. Not far from Minet el-Beida a storm forced the boat into a small bay for protection from the weather; Schaeffer and Chenet sat up all night to protect their precious goods from other dangers. The following day they arrived back in Latakia.

In retrospect, it would seem natural that such a remarkable discovery would have quickly captured the attention of the media, but such was not initially the case. On May 21, 1929, a week after the discovery of the first clay tablet, a very brief progress report of the excavations at Minet el-Beida appeared on page thirteen of the London *Times*. Five months later, on page fifteen of the October 22nd issue of the *Times*, an equally short item appeared, reporting the apparent discovery of the cuneiform alphabet. There were scholars at that time who were very interested indeed in the discovery, but the larger public interest was not to be captured until the attempts at deciphering the formerly unknown alphabetic script began.

The decipherment of an unknown writing system is not an easy task and requires a particular kind of skill, backed up by long training and extensive knowledge. The extraordinary feature of the discoveries at Ras Shamra is that the script was deciphered, virtually independently, by three different scholars. Pride of place must go to the linguist Charles Virolleaud, for a number of reasons. Schaeffer had entrusted the first clay tablets to Virolleaud for a report and examination; the linguist published his first report on the tablets in volume 10 of the periodical *Syria*, in late 1929. Apart from his learned observations, Virolleaud performed a remarkable and unusual service in this report; he included excellent hand copies of the forty-eight tablets and fragments in alphabetic cuneiform, thus making the texts accessible to other scholars for examination. This was a generous and unselfish act, in striking contrast to that of a British scholar, Sir Arthur Evans, who had kept some tablets discovered in Crete in his own possession for many years, hoping thereby to retain for himself the honor of decipherment.

Not only did Virolleaud publish copies of the texts, but he also made a number of suggestions in his first report (elaborated in a more detailed report in 1931) which were to prove invaluable to the process of deciphering the script. He noted that the writing system was alphabetic and that words were separated by a small vertical wedge shape (ᵧ). The identification of the word divider was important, for it enabled him to recognize that most words were short, consisting of only three or four letters; the shortness of the words made it highly unlikely that the language concealed by the script was Greek or an ancient relative of Greek.

Virolleaud and the two other decipherers reached their solutions by different methods, and although Virolleaud was not the first to solve the problem of decipherment completely, a brief look at his method indicates the technique he employed. He began with the single letter word which he had noticed on an axe head, and combined that observation with the strong probability that the language underlying the script was a Semitic language, akin to Hebrew or Phoenician. The occurrence of this single-letter word, both on an axe head and at the beginning of one of the inscribed tablets, suggested to him that the word was a preposition. The preposition "to" was most likely, as archaeological and linguistic analogies suggested to him; in Hebrew, Arabic, or Phoenician, the preposition "to" would be the single consonant *l*. Therefore, Virolleaud's starting point was that the symbol 𝍍 = *l*.

Then he grouped together all words employing the single symbol that had been identified in a preliminary fashion. In his description of the process some of the steps are missing, but it is clear that he began looking for the equivalent of the word "king," which is spelled consonantally as *mlk* in almost all Semitic languages. The search was reasonable, for it had already been established that the city had been ruled by kings in ancient times, as indicated by the discovery of royal tombs in the vicinity of Minet el-Beida.

He was successful in finding a word that he thought mean king (see *Figure 5*) and thus had preliminary identifications of the symbols representing the letters *m*, *l*, and *k*. When he found the same word with a fourth sign attached, and the fourth sign was identical to the first (*mlkm*), he had achieved a partial degree of confirmation; the letter *m* in some Semitic languages commonly functions as a plural termination (as does *s* in English), hence the symbols transliterated as *mlkm* would seem to mean "kings."

Virolleaud continued to work on a speculative basis, still depending on the data that were reasonably firm: ⫟ = *l* and ⊢⫟ = *m*. He identified the name *Baal* (see *Figure 5*), a well-known Canaanite god, and when the same name appeared with a fourth letter added, but not the plural termination *m*, he concluded that the fourth letter must be the femine termination, *t*. Then he found a three-letter word having *l* as the middle symbol, but the first and third signs were identical. Such a combination of signs is rare in the spelling of Semitic words, the only common example being šlš "three" (to employ the Hebrew spelling). So, still working on a speculative basis, he had a provisional identification of the symbol for š; and when the same three-letter word was found with the *m* sign at the end, he concluded it must be šlšm "thirty," still basing his speculation on the commonality of certain basic words in the Semitic languages. (Later, this particular identification was to be modified, for though Virolleaud was correct in his identification of the word, it is spelled *tlt* in Ugaritic; but the principle on which he was operating was sound.) He continued from these initial results, making assumptions, testing them, and gradually increasing the knowledge of the values to be given to each symbol.

But Virolleaud was not the only scholar engaged in the process of decipherment; though pride of place goes to him, the honor of the speediest decipherment goest to Hans Bauer, a fifty-one-year-old professor of oriental languages from the German University of Halle. Bauer was a man of rare brilliance, having studied for a while at the Gregorian University in Rome; then he continued with the advanced study of oriental languages at the Universities of Leipzig and Berlin. In addition to having mastered several European and Semitic languages, he was conversant with various

FIGURE 5: Virolleaud's preliminary steps in decipherment

Stage 1   𝕄 = *l* (preposition: "to, for")

Stage 2   ⟊ 𝕄 ⊳- = *mlk* ("king")

Stage 3   ⟊ 𝕄 ⊳-⟊ = *mlkm* ("kings")

Stage 4   𝕏 ⟨ 𝕄 = *b'l* ("Baal")

                𝕏 ⟨ 𝕄 ⟊ = *b'lm* ("Baals")

Stage 5   ⟊ 𝕄 ⟊ = *ṯlṯ* ("three")

East Asian languages; his background had also been enriched by experience of cryptanalytical work with the German armed forces during World War I. On April 22, 1930, Bauer received a copy of Virolleaud's transcriptions of the alphabetic cuneiform texts, and immediately he set to work. Within five days he had assigned values to twenty of the alphabetic symbols, employing a technique (common to cryptanalysis in military work) which was initially statistical. He reported his success to the French on April 28 and a report appeared in the journal *Syria* in mid-1930. Bauer himself published a preliminary report in the *Vossische Zeitung* of June 4, 1930.

Bauer's method was thoroughly systematic and depended to a considerable extent on statistical data and probabilities. Working on the assumption that the language lying beneath the script was Semitic, and therefore a language in which words were developed by means of prefixes and suffixes, he compiled several lists of signs. First, he compiled lists of signs that commonly began words (prefixes), then those that commonly concluded words (suffixes), and finally signs that appeared to be able to function as single-letter words (see *Figure 6*). Turning to the other end of the problem, he listed letters commonly used as prefixes in the known Semitic languages (e.g., Phoenician, Hebrew), then those commonly used as suffixes, and finally letters that could function independently as words. These lists provided the basis for the next stage of his operation.

Comparing both sets of lists, Bauer noted that two cuneiform signs were common to all three categories (prefixes, suffixes, and single-letter words), and that three letters (one of which could be eliminated on statistical grounds as improbable) occurred in all three of these categories in known Semitic languages. On this basis, he arrived at his first preliminary identifications of the values of two signs, the letters *w* and *m*. From there, by a process of development and refinement, he was able eventually — within a period of less than one week — to assign preliminary values to approximately three-quarters of the cuneiform signs.

While Bauer was making progress in Germany, another French scholar, Édouard Dhorme, was working on the problem in Jerusalem. Dhorme was a senior scholar, born in 1881, who had already published numerous works on Near Eastern and biblical matters. Like Bauer, he had worked in cryptanalysis during the First World War, serving with French intelligence in Saloniki, Greece. Apart from his period of military service, Dhorme had been on the staff of the École Biblique in Jerusalem since 1904 and was thoroughly conversant with Semitic languages. Dhorme initially had only limited success; in fact, quite unfairly, the London *Times* correspondent in Beirut, in an article in the December 20, 1930, issue, said he had been unsuccessful. Though his success was initially limited, William F. Albright, the distinguished American archaeologist, alerted Dhorme to Bauer's preliminary article in the *Vossische Zeitung*. From that general article, he made a number of minor corrections in his own system, and then, in correspondence with Bauer, was able to accelerate progress towards a complete solution.

It was Virolleaud who had made the first steps, and in some ways Virolleaud also added the finishing touches at the end, after the brilliant advances of Bauer and Dhorme. Virolleaud had been about to publish his initial results in May 1930, when he heard that Bauer had claimed the decipherment. On August 20, the same year, he received both Bauer's study and also the newly discovered texts which Schaeffer had unearthed in his second season (see below). He thus had two new sets of data with which to work. The newly arrived clay tablets were covered with sediment, and Virolleaud entrusted them to a technician, M. André, for cleaning. It was not until September 20, 1930, that he was able to examine the new texts. After fours days of work, utilizing this

FIGURE 6: **Stages in the process of Bauer's decipherment**

Stage 1 Common prefixes, suffixes, and single-letter words

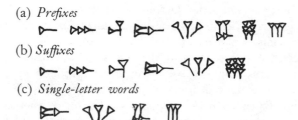

(a) *Prefixes*

(b) *Suffixes*

(c) *Single-letter words*

Stage 2 If the language was Semitic:
(a) *Prefixes must include:* ', *y*, *m*, *n*, *t* (and possibly *b*, *h*, *w*, *k*, *l*).
(b) *Suffixes must include:* *h*, *k*, *m*, *n*, *t* (and possibly *w* and *y*).
(c) *Single-letter words:* *l*, *m* (and possibly *b*, *k*, *w*).

Stage 3 (i) All three sign groups include 𒁺 and 𒀉
(ii) All three alphabetical lists include *w*, *k*, *m*
(iii) tentatively eliminate *k;*
(iv) 𒁺 = *w* or *m;* 𒀉 = *w* or *m*

Subsequent stages: similar process of elimination applied to groups (a) and (b), leading to further tentative identifications, which are then tested in word formations.

---

new material, Virolleaud was able to confirm a large number of earlier identifications and to establish the value of certain letters which had still been unknown prior to that time. He communicated his final results in a letter to René Dussaud which was read to l'Académie in Paris on October 3, 1930. Three weeks later, on October 24, Virolleaud presented his decipherment in person to l'Académie; at almost precisely the same time, Hans Bauer published his final results ("Die Entzifferung der Keilschriftalphabets von Ras Shamra," 1930) and Dhorme published a brief statement of his results in the periodical *Revue Biblique*.

In the spring of 1930, while these three scholars were setting about the process of deciphering an unknown script, Schaeffer had returned to Syria to begin his second season of excavation. On this second expedition, he took his wife and daughter along with him. The second campaign extended from March 20 to June 19, and on this occasion, no doubt as a result of the first season's success, it received fuller support. Now Schaeffer had sufficient funds to employ some 250 local diggers, and General de Bigault du Granrut assigned a larger detachment of thirty soldiers for protection of the expedition. In a project of this size, the possibility of valuable items being stolen from the site by the workers was increased. Schaeffer attempted to overcome the problem in an ingenious fashion; he hired both local Alaouites and also persons of a Turkish background from further north. He mixed the Alaouites and Turks together; as the two groups did not like each other, he hoped that if a member of one group stole something, a member of the other group would report. It was a wise precaution, given the value of some of the objects which were to be discovered before the season ended.

The first few days were spent in a reexamination of the tombs at Minet el-Beida which had been discovered in 1929. Then, at the end of March, new excavations began in the general area of the necropolis. The most interesting discovery in this area was a large building; when it was uncovered, it was seen to have thirty-six rooms, numerous corridors, and several wells, but it was apparently not a building that had been used for normal residence. It was connected by underground tunnel to a royal tomb, and was a facility apparently provided for the "use" of deceased kings. Numerous valuable objects were found in the rooms of this mortuary palace that provided further indication of the culture and wealth of the royal families.

After six weeks of excavation at Minet el-Beida, Schaeffer transferred his work crew once again to the large tell, Ras Shamra; there he began to dig once again in the vicinity of the library or school, where the clay tablets had been discovered the previous year. He began by sinking a deep probe and discovered that the floor of the library (which was dated to about the fifteenth-twelfth centuries B.C.) was not built on virgin soil. Beneath the library floors was evidence of another level of settlement; he found objects indicating that the area had been a cemetery, dating approximately to the twenty-first— sixteenth centuries. Below the cemetery there was evidence of a still more ancient level of settlement, dating from the early or middle third millennium.

After establishing the antiquity of the mound as a place of human residence, Schaeffer redirected the attention of his team to the library/school building. Here, further clay tablets were discovered, many of them in the cuneiform alphabet; several were impressive by virtue of their size and the fact that they contained three separate columns of writing. There were other texts of importance, including syllabaries and a bilingual lexicon. It was becoming clear to Schaeffer that the civilization he was rediscovering had been multilingual. In 1930 he estimated that four languages had been in use in this ancient city; three years later, he revised his estimate to eight languages (*Figure 7*).

In addition to texts, real treasure was found in the library area.

FIGURE 7: Languages and scripts used in ancient Ugarit

LANGUAGE	SCRIPT OF TEXTS
Akkadian Texts	Cuneiform
Sumerian Texts	Cuneiform
Hurrian Texts	Cuneiform
Hittite Texts	Cuneiform
Ugaritic Texts	Alphabetic Cuneiform
Hurrian Texts	Alphabetic Cuneiform
Akkadian Texts	Alphabetic Cuneiform
Egyptian Texts	Hieroglyphic
Hittite Texts	(Hittite) Hieroglyphic
Cypro-Minoan Texts	Local Cypro-Minoan Script

The data shown here indicate a more advanced knowledge
of language and texts than was available to
Schaeffer between 1930 and 1933.

Underneath the library steps were lodged silver vessels and vases that were of considerable weight. The weight came from their contents, for the vessels were filled with many gold and silver objects, rings and trinkets.

By the end of 1930 a good deal was known about the ancient city located on the Syrian coast. Two seasons of excavation had resulted in a rich harvest of ancient artifacts, and buildings had been uncovered in both the city area and the nearby necropolis. In addition to the physical remains there were written texts, and the decipherment of the script by late 1930 meant that these texts could now be read. The content of the texts would fill out more abundantly the picture of life as it had been in that ancient city. But still, in 1930, the name of the city was not known.

In his report of the second excavation Schaeffer had ventured a suggestion. Perhaps the ancient city had been called Ṣapuna; the name appeared, for example, in conjunction with the divine name Baal on the Egyptian object discovered in the temple area. The difficulty with this suggestion was that there was no external evidence to support the existence, in ancient times, of a city called Ṣapuna in that region. An American scholar, in a learned footnote to an article published in 1931 in the journal *Archiv für Orient-forschung*, suggested another possibility; W. F. Albright suggested that the name of the city might have been Ugarit. He referred to numerous second millennium texts from other areas of the Near East that indicated the existence of such a city in Syria or Palestine, but by 1930 no city with that name had been identified. He promised to write an article in support of his hypothesis, but as it turned out, the article was unnecessary. As Virolleaud translated the newly discovered texts from Ras Shamra, it was found that the name Ugarit (*'ugrt*) was present in several of the texts; one text even referred to a certain *NQMD*, who was "King of Ugarit." Once this certain identification had been made, the name Ugarit gradually began to replace Ras Shamra (the modern Arabic place name) in writings about the ancient city. The newly discovered alphabetic script, and the newly discovered language which it conveyed, were designated Ugaritic.

The excavations continued. Before the outbreak of the Second World War, a total of eleven campaigns were conducted under Schaeffer's leadership in the vicinity of Minet el-Beida and Ras Shamra. For all the massive amount of work over a period of more than ten years, much still remained to be done; only about one-eighth of the surface of Ras Shamra had been uncovered (and that mostly at one level) and only about one-sixth of the area at Minet el-Beida. The tenth campaign was conducted in the autumn of 1938, the eleventh in the winter (February 1939), and then world conflict enforced a suspension of activity for several years. The chief excavator, Schaeffer, was to turn to other duties for a number of years; from 1940-1945 he served as captain of corvette in the Free French Naval Forces.

Although eleven campaigns had not exhausted the possibilities of the two sites, nevertheless an enormous amount of knowledge had been gained. There were, in 1939, considerably more than 150 texts in alphabetic cuneiform, some of them very long. There were also numerous texts in other languages. Important parts of the ancient city had been pinpointed: a temple of Baal, a temple of Dagan, portions of a palace, a library, numerous private houses, and streets. Parts of the neighboring seaport town and necropolis were also known.

After the Second World War, a new series of archaeological campaigns began at Ras Shamra; the first two postwar campaigns (the twelfth campaign in 1948 and the thirteenth in 1949) were essentially limited operations, developing further a few new areas of the site, but focusing primarily on the consolidation of what had been left untouched during the war years and almost a decade of archaeological inactivity. But full-scale excavations began again in 1950; they continued to be directed by Claude Schaeffer, up to and including the thirty-first campaign in 1969. Since then, the continuing excavations have been directed by Henri de Contenson (1971-1973), Adnan Bounni, Nassib Saliby, Jacques and Elisabeth Lagarce (codirectors, 1974), and Jean-Claude Margueron (1975-1976). After a short lapse in the series of campaigns, Marguerite Yon of the University of Lyons, France, was appointed the new director of the French mission in 1978 and remains currently responsible for the excavation of the site.

The postwar excavations have developed still further various areas of the tell, uncovering an enormous palace (known only in a preliminary fashion prior to the war), a residential area of the city, a special artisans' quarter, and various larger homes that once belonged to the leading citizens of the ancient city. Archives were found not only in the palace and temple areas, but also in the homes of certain individual persons who had once participated actively in the life of the city. A few short documents were also discovered in the port town adjoining the capital city of Ugarit. It is on the basis of many years of excavation, and the extensive finds of the archaeologists, that it is possible to reconstruct in a tentative fashion what life and civilization must have been like in Ugarit.

Chapter III:
LIFE IN
ANCIENT UGARIT

THE city of Ugarit died more than three millennia in the past; its life and civilization came abruptly to an end and the city was never rebuilt. But from the ruins and remains which have been excavated so carefully by the French archaeologists, it is possible to reconstruct in part the life of that ancient city. The remains of buildings, the artifacts, and above all the written texts provide the raw material from which to construct an account of the nature of life in the ancient kingdom of Ugarit.

The focus in this reconstruction of life in Ugarit will be upon the last two centuries of its history (fourteenth-thirteenth centuries B.C.), for those are the centuries which overlap with the beginning of the biblical period. But the city came into existence long before the beginnings of biblical history. The location of the city was a natural one for human settlement, and archaeologists have found evidence of human habitation going back to the fifth millennium. The evidence from the lowest level of settlement, level V (see *Figure 8*, below), indicates that the first settlers belonged to a Neolithic culture. Above that level was found evidence of a settlement of the Chalcolithic type (level IV); above that again were found the remains of a settlement in the Early Bronze Age (level III), at which time there were apparently strong links with the culture and civilization of Mesopotamia (modern Iraq). But it is the last two levels which are most pertinent. It was probably during the Middle Bronze Age (level II) that the city began to assume its place as a significant port and capital of a small kingdom. Level I, the highest of the levels of permanent settlement, reflects the culture of the Late Bronze Age, and it is this level which is of primary interest for the early biblical period. After level I, no evidence has been found of any permanent settlement on a large scale; there were apparently only sporadic and semi-

26

permanent settlements on the tell and in the bay area after the Late Bronze Age.

Not only is level I the most significant for the present inquiry; it is also the level providing the most complete sources of information. It is thus possible to know more about life in ancient Ugarit during the Late Bronze Age than it is about life in the earlier periods. But any kind of reconstruction on the basis of archaeological findings must be undertaken with care. The evidence is rarely complete; physical objects are often broken, and written texts are often scarcely legible, or are broken and incomplete at critical points. Despite all the difficulties, it is possible to take the bits of evidence and piece them together like the parts of a jigsaw puzzle. Some pieces are missing and may never be found, but enough have survived to provide a picture of what life must have been like for the citizens of Ugarit in the fourteenth and thirteenth centuries B.C.

A geographical description of the city of Ugarit and its territories provides an appropriate starting point. The city of Ugarit, capital of the small kingdom, was located close to the Mediterranean coast. During its Golden Age (fourteenth-thirteenth centuries), it controlled a territory of approximately thirteen hundred square miles. The northern border was located near Jebel el-ʿAqra

FIGURE 8: Stratification levels at Ras Shamra

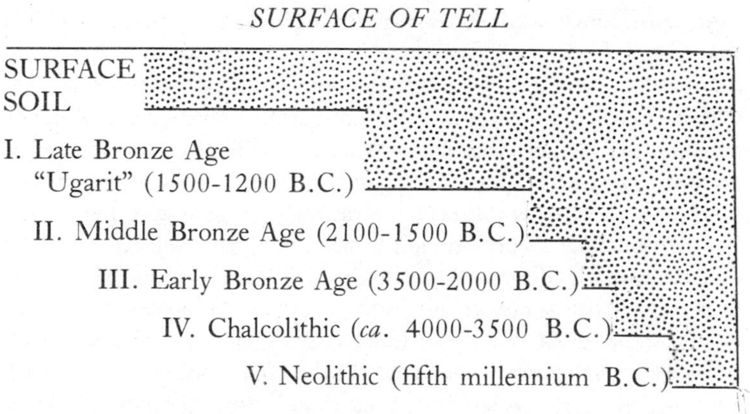

SURFACE OF TELL

SURFACE
SOIL

I. Late Bronze Age
   "Ugarit" (1500-1200 B.C.)

   II. Middle Bronze Age (2100-1500 B.C.)

      III. Early Bronze Age (3500-2000 B.C.)

         IV. Chalcolithic (*ca.* 4000-3500 B.C.)

            V. Neolithic (fifth millennium B.C.)

(the mountain northeast of the city, called Mt. Ṣapan in Ugaritic and Mt. Casius in later classical times). Inland, to the east, Ugarit's territories may have extended some twenty or thirty miles from the Mediterranean coast. The southern border was probably in the vicinity of Tell Sukas (Shuksi); alternatively, it may have been marked at the spot where the short river, Nahr as-Senn, flows into the sea.

The territory controlled by the city state of Ugarit was relatively compact and self-sufficient. The ocean formed a natural border on the west, while the eastern border was marked by a chain of mountains running north and south, separating the coastal plain from the interior of modern Syria. This coastal chain of mountains reaches an average height of about 3608 feet, the highest point being 5141 feet. The territory around the city itself is in the form of a plain, but north of the plain the land begins to rise gradually into the rocky country that forms the foothills, culminating in Jebel el-'Aqra, at a height of 5840 feet.

There was only one river of any size in the territory, now called Nahr al-Kabir; it follows from the north to the south, entering the Mediterranean just south of the modern city of Latakia. There were a few small rivers, though they were insufficient for the development of great irrigation systems, as was done in Egypt and Mesopotamia. But most of the territory was usable as farmland without the benefits of irrigation. And, in contrast to the modern situation, the land was more heavily forested during the time when the kingdom of Ugarit flourished, especially on the slopes of Mt. Ṣapan. The pleasantness of this ancient Mediterranean state benefited still further from a mild and moderate climate. There was normally sufficient rainfall (about thirty inches per annum) to meet the needs of farmers, though farmers have always worried about the adequacy of the rainfall! One of the central themes in native religion within the state was the desire for the god Baal to provide adequate rain so that the crops might flourish and the harvest be adequate. The kingdom of Ugarit could have been a very pleasant place in which to live, self-sufficient on the basis of an agriculture economy. It was much more than that, however, and it was the city's strategic location on the Mediterranean coast which contributed to its short-lived glory.

The main section of the city itself covered an area of approximately fifty acres; that is not large by the standards of modern sprawling cities, but within the fortifications of the ancient city many of the houses were built closely together. In the northern part of the city, standing on slightly higher ground than the other buildings, were located two large temples, one for Baal and one for Dagan. Between the temples there was a priest's house containing a library which probably served a dual role as a scribal school. Immediately south of the temples, and still on higher ground, was the upper town, its streets lined with houses of considerable proportions.

In the western section of the city was the royal palace. The palace complex was very large, indicative of the wealth of the city during its Golden Age. It served as more than a residence for the royal family; the several large archives found within the complex indicate that it functioned also as the kingdom's administrative center. The palace seems to have been a relatively small building initially; as the prosperity of the successive kings increased, additions were constructed around the original building until the whole complex reached massive proportions. The total area occupied by the palace has been estimated at almost 2.5 acres. It had some ninety rooms, five large courtyards, a dozen staircases leading to the upper floor, and an interior garden. There were some wells within the palace, and additional wells outside it from which water was fed into the palace through an aqueduct system.

Many of the homes and buildings in the city provide evidence that not all wealth was confined to the royal family. For example, one large house which belonged to a leading citizen called Rapanou had thirty-four rooms, including a library containing an impressive variety of written texts. Rapanou appears to have been a leading official in the court of Ammistamru III. In Rapanou's house, as in many others, a family vault or sepulchre was located under the house or the courtyard and may indicate that the commemoration and veneration of the dead was a significant aspect of family religion. Several buildings contained private archives, quite separate from those of the palace or priestly establishment. Such private archives may have belonged to scribes, several of whom held high office in society; they were equivalent in general terms to senior civil servants in modern forms of government. In addition to the great palace in the western section of the city, there was a smaller palace (perhaps a former royal establishment) just to the east of the main palace.

FIGURE 9: Ras Shamra: Buildings on the tell

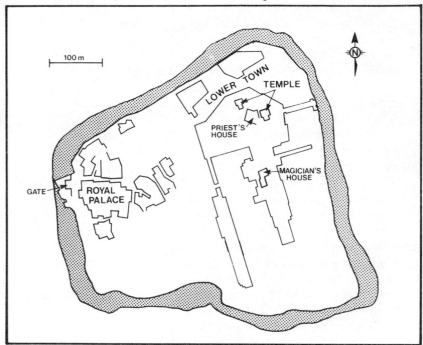

Less than a mile west of the city, built on the southern shore of the bay now called Minet el-Beida, was Ugarit's port town (probably called Ma'ḫāzu). The port town was much smaller than the main city; it had a waterfront area facing northwards across the bay, and other houses were clustered to the south of the waterfront. Further round the bay, to the east, was the large cemetery or necropolis area, which served both the port and the city of Ugarit. The port at Minet el-Beida was not the kingdom's only access to the Mediterranean's trade routes. Three other ports were known: Attalig, Gib'ala, and Ḫimuli (probably located on Pigeon Island, to the north of Ugarit; today the island is very small, about 150 meters long and thirty meters wide, but it may have been slightly larger in ancient times). Although these ports functioned primarily as trading centers, they may also have served as a base for the fishing industry.

A large portion of the population of the state lived outside the city and the port town. They lived in the many rural villages which constituted a significant part of the kingdom's population and economy. There were approximately two hundred such villages in the kingdom, most of which are known by name though their location can rarely be specified with any certainty. All the villages were small by modern standards, with an average population of a little more than one hundred. Nevertheless, they were vital to the kingdom's economy, for their inhabitants were engaged in agriculture, forestry, and cattle raising; they provided the necessary staples for the population as a whole. The total population of the rural communities has been estimated at around twenty-five thousand, which may have been more than one-third of the population of the state.

The government of Ugarit was in the hands of the royal family, which normally functioned as a hereditary monarchy. Many of the documents from the city archives, and especially from the archives in the royal palace, illuminate partially the history of the monarchy during the Golden Age of Ugarit. The roots of the monarchy, however, stretched far back into the city's history to about the beginning of the second millennium. Two kings are known from this early period: Niqmadu I and his son, Yaqarum. Little is known of them beyond their names, but it is possible that they were the progenitors of the royal dynasty which reappeared during the Golden Age.

The Golden Age proper may be said to begin with the reign of Ammistamru III (*ca.* 1390-1360 B.C.). While internal affairs in Ugarit seem to have posed little difficulty, Ammistamru faced a major problem in external affairs, which all his successors also had to face. He lived in a world of imperial powers: the super powers of the time were the Hittite Empire in Anatolia to the north (modern Turkey), and Egypt to the south. These super powers were not friendly toward each other, though the kingdom of Ugarit prospered most when the balance of power between them was approximately equal. And the super powers benefited from the presence of Ugarit, partly because it formed a buffer state between them, and partly because it offered relatively neutral ground on which to undertake international trade. The location and role of Ugarit on the Mediterranean coast had certain parallels to the location and role of Beirut in the twentieth century, prior to the outbreak of civil war in the 1970s.

Both Ammistamru III and Niqmadu III (in the early part of

FIGURE 10: Monarchs during Ugarit's Golden Age

MONARCH	APPROXIMATE DATE
'AMMISTAMRU III	1380
NIQMADU III	1360
ARḤALBU II	
NIQMEPA VI	1300
AMMISTAMRU IV	
IBIRANU VI	
NIQMADU IV	
'AMMURAPI III	1200

Based on the study of K. A. Kitchen, "The King List of Ugarit," *Ugarit-Forschungen* 9 (1977): 131-142.

---

his reign) enjoyed friendly relations with Egypt. They attempted also to maintain a good relationship with the Hittites, though the closeness of the mighty Hittite Empire introduced the element of fear into that relationship. During the reign of Niqmadu III, Ugarit, through no fault of its own, became a vassal state of the Hittite Empire. Two Hittite colonies to the northeast of Ugarit, Nukhash and Mukish, had joined in a rebellion against the Hittite emperor Suppiluliumas. The kingdom of Ugarit refused their suggestions of joining the rebellion and as a consequence lost control of certain of its territories to the rebels. There is some evidence to suggest that a part of Ugarit's royal palace was burned down during the resulting conflict. The rebellion was put down by the emperor Suppiluliumas, and it was then that Ugarit became a vassal state of the Hittite Empire. The vassal treaty was not entirely disadvantageous, however; the emperor transferred to Ugarit's control certain territories which had formerly belonged to the rebel states. Later in Niqmadu's reign there was a further rebellion in Nukhash; the Ugaritic king mustered his army and used it to help the new Hittite king, Mursilis II, in quelling the rebellion. There is some evidence, though, that Ugarit's strength had grown by this time and that helping the Hittites was as much a matter of self-interest as it was a matter of fulfilling treaty obligations.

Niqmadu's son, Arḫalbu, has a name which is Hurrian in form, rather than the native Semitic of Ugarit; it is possible that he had a Hurrian mother. His rise to power may indicate a temporary growth of Hurrian influence in the kingdom. The Hurrians, who at that time were settled mainly in southeastern Anatolia, had been present in Ugarit for a long time and may even have ruled the city for a while before the fourteenth century B.C. But Arḫalbu, who paid little attention to his duties toward the Hittites, held the throne for less than ten years. When the Hittites regained effective control of Ugarit, they replaced Arḫalbu by his brother (presumably a half brother) Niqmepa VI, who in turn represents a return to the native Semitic tradition in the royal family of Ugarit. Niqmepa appears to have brought internal affairs firmly under control; in external matters, the Hittites retained firm authority.

Only a little is known of the reign of Ammistamru IV, Niqmepa's son. Internally, he appears to have suffered from family quarrels, partly with his brothers and partly as a result of his divorce of a wife, who was related to the royal family in the neighboring state of the Amurru. His successors, Ibiranu and Niqmadu IV, are also little known. But throughout the thirteenth century certain major changes were taking place in international affairs; for a while they appeared to be to Ugarit's advantage, though eventually they spelled disaster for the city. The Hittite Empire was in a state of gradual decline; the initial consequence for Ugarit was greater freedom, and in part that freedom was exploited in more positive relationships with Egypt. But in the west, a new threat was beginning to emerge in the person of the "Sea Peoples" (see below).

The kings of Ugarit were able to acquire for themselves considerable wealth, together with the power that wealth could buy. The great palace complex signifies the possession of personal wealth, achieved through trade and various systems of taxation. But the king's power rested in his government and personal retainers, who could be paid in money and rewarded in property for their services to the king. Although wealth and power can corrupt, there was a noble ideal of kingship in Ugarit which helped to guard against corruption. The king was a man of responsibility. It was a royal virtue to give attention to the needs of the weak and oppressed; he was expected to protect the rights of widows, orphans, and other socially disadvantaged persons. And he shared also in responsibility for the judicial system of the state. The extent to which individual kings lived up to the grand ideals is not known with any certainty, but the existence of such ideals speaks well for the civilization of Ugarit.

The king maintained control of the internal and external affairs of state by means of his armed forces, a standing army and a permanent navy. Both were of considerable size, and military personnel were an important segment in the mosaic of Ugarit's society. The two basic divisions of the army were the infantry and chariotry, of which the former was numerically the larger. Infantrymen were well equipped with weapons such as lances, slings, and shields; some infantry divisions may have been constituted entirely of archers. The chariot troops, though numerically smaller, were more powerful in military operations (the equivalent of tank regiments in modern ground warfare). The chariots were manned mainly by the *maryannu*, a special class of chariot warriors who received and perpetuated their military profession in a hereditary tradition. They were supported by grooms and others who cared for the chariots and horses. The strength of the standing army was supplemented by a system of conscription; each village in the kingdom had to supply a number of able-bodied men on a regular basis for military service. In times of war, the army could be strengthened still further by a general conscription.

As a maritime and mercantile power, Ugarit also required a navy; the navy provided the necessary protection for merchant vessels, but more importantly was used in defense of the state in times of war. The size of the navy is not known with certainty, but during the thirteenth century it appears to have been very large relative to the size of the kingdom. One letter, dated during the very last days of the kingdom of Ugarit, refers to the preparation of 150 ships as reinforcements for the navy's principal fleet. If reinforcements numbered 150, the fleet itself may have been at least twice that size. The navy, like the army, could be strengthened by means of conscription; it is possible that naval conscripts were drawn from the coastal towns, where men would already have seagoing experience on merchant and fishing vessels.

Religious personnel constituted a further significant grouping in the city of Ugarit. The temples of Dagan and Baal dominated the city in their physical location, and in size they were second only to the great palace. Such temples required a large number of support staff. The services of the temple were maintained by the priests, of whom there were many. The chief priest was responsible for the temple establishment, its administration, and certain religious duties. Under him there were numerous priests grouped according to families; one administrative text refers to twelve distinct families of priests. The priests received a portion of their income and support through their service in the temples, but in addition many owned land; in some cases it had been given as a royal grant. The priests as a whole, and the chief priest in particular, were also responsible for the preservation and transmission of the religious and literary classics of the state. One version of the great myth of Baal cites the chief priest, called 'Atnprln, as its authority. And it is significant that some of the most important religious and literary texts come from the temple and priestly archives, indicating further the role of the priests as scribes and librarians. Priests also had a military function, as is clear from references to them in administrative texts describing auxiliary military personnel; they are also listed in an army payroll text. Their role was that of support personnel, providing advice of a religious or oracular nature to military commanders. They were, in other words, an intelligence corps, purporting to provide divine counsel with respect to strategy and military operations; they were not primarily chaplains!

In addition to priests, there was a further group of religious persons called "holy ones" or "devotees." There is only clear evidence of male personnel in this category, though there may also have been female "devotees." The function of these people may have been related in some way to sexual activity in the temple. They are sometimes referred to in other sources as "sacred prostitutes," though such a designation does not reflect an objective attitude towards their religious activity. Their role in worship was related intimately to the activities of a fertility religion, in which it was believed that the fertility of the land depended upon the fertility of the gods; the sexual act in the context of such worship was intended to secure the fertility of the gods, and hence of the land.

A major religious establishment such as that of Ugarit required not only primary religious functionaries but also support person-nel. The support tasks varied from the mundane duty of cleaning and maintaining the premises to the more religious duties of help-ing the priests in their sacrifices and offerings. Such duties were assumed by a large group of persons referred to as "temple ser-vitors"; one administrative text lists by name some sixty such ser-vitors. Further support was provided by professional musicians, who provided the musical accompaniment for the temple's wor-ship; they included both instrumentalists and singers.

Not all religious activities were confined to the city of Ugarit, although it seems probable that the worship in the two city temples functioned as a type of state religion. Outside the city, there were religious shrines and sanctuaries in many of the villages, and these were supported and maintained by their own local priests. Al-though the villagers had certain responsibilities toward the state religion, their primary religious life was at the local shrine or sanctuary, maintained by local priests.

The city of Ugarit, like any cosmopolitan city, had a richly diverse population. A colony of foreign merchants and diplomats resided there, functioning both in the context of trade and dip-lomatic relationships. Egypt and the Hittite Empire were repre-sented by merchant companies, ambassadors, and diplomats at various periods during Ugarit's Golden Age. People from Cyprus (Alashiya) and Crete were also present; the Cretans frequently built their homes in the native Cretan style, rather than according to local custom. Other foreign residents came from the various Mesopotamian states situated to the east of Ugarit.

Apart from those who were formally aliens or foreign repre-sentatives, the standard population of the city were extraordinarily diverse (the village populations, by contrast, were more uniformly "Ugaritan" or Semitic). The regular city population, in addition to native peoples and Syrians in general, included Hurrians, Cyp-riotes, Cretans, Hittites, Egyptians, Achaeans, and others. This ethnic diversity and cosmopolitan character is reflected in part in the multiplicity of languages contained in the texts which have been recovered from the city's archives, which include principally Ugaritic (the native language of the state), Akkadian (a significant language for trade and international relations), Hurrian (a non-Semitic language, used in northern Mesopotamia and southeastern Anatolia), Hittite, Egyptian, and Cypriote. While many of the languages would have been used primarily for official purposes, others, such as Hurrian, may have been used alongside Ugaritic in everyday life. Thus, ethnically and linguistically, Ugarit was a real "city of Babel," but for all that, it appears to have had a relatively harmonious inner life. The absence of ethnic and inter-religious strife is in part a reflection of the cosmopolitan character of the city, and in part a reflection of the flexibility of the syncre-tistic nature of the various religions which coexisted in Ugarit.

The internal economy of the state was based upon agriculture and a local manufacturing industry. Agriculture was diversified. Crops included cereals, grapes, and olives; from the latter two, wine and oil were produced. The natural supply of timber was harvested and provided the necessary raw material for both con-struction and shipbuilding; there was sufficient timber for export to places such as Egypt, which lacked natural resources of timber. Sheep and cattle were kept, contributing wool and meat to the economy. The manufacturing industry included the production of textiles and weapons. With respect to textiles, both garments and materials of linen and wool were produced for internal use and for export purposes; the use of distinctive dyes contributed to the production of highly valued materials such as expensive purple wools and fabrics. Swordsmiths produced weapons, such as bronze longswords, some of which were exported to Egypt. Metalworkers manufactured vessels of considerable beauty from metals such as bronze and gold.

This healthy internal economy contributed to the king's wealth through a system of taxation. Taxes and tithes were attached to the production of grain, wine, olive oil, beef, and other commodities; they were sometimes paid in money, sometimes in kind. Severe penalties were attached to the nonpayment of taxes. In this way, the health of the economy contributed directly to the wealth of the royal establishment. The king could also employ a system of in-direct taxation, namely the *corvée* (a system of forced labor), to draw from men their services in the direct working of a royal land or land belonging to his close retainers.

It was trade, however, which contributed to the real wealth and influence of Ugarit to a far greater extent than did the state's natural resources and internal economy. The possibility of major international trade was partly the accident — or blessing — of ge-ography. Ugarit's location on the Mediterranean coast provided an avenue to the Mediterranean sea routes, but also access from those routes to the interior. The geographical fact, combined with the location of Ugarit between the two great empires of the time, Egypt and the Hittite Empire, provided the state with an ideal opportunity to dominate trade in the area of the eastern Mediterranean. During the Golden Age, that opportunity was seized and fully exploited; what Beirut has been in the twentieth century, Ugarit was in the past.

Overland routes carried goods in and out of Ugarit; these routes linked the city with Anatolia (the Hittite Empire), with various internal states in Syria and Mesopotamia, with other areas in Syria and Palestine, and with Egypt in the south. Trade by land was conducted by means of large donkey caravans; donkeys were an expensive and vital commodity in a trading nation like Ugarit. One economic text refers to the purchase of some four hundred donkeys, an indication of the size and significance of the caravans. But of even greater significance than the overland routes were the maritime routes, linking Ugarit's harbor with the whole of the eastern Mediterranean world. Some of the sea routes linked Ugarit with places already accessible by the overland routes, but the use of seagoing transportation was preferred when it was available. The sending of goods by sea was generally cheaper than by donkey caravans; in addition, larger and heavier quantities of goods could more easily be transported on the maritime routes. By means of its sea routes, Ugarit engaged in trade with ports on the eastern Mediterranean coast (such as Byblos, Tyre, and Acco), with Egypt, with Cyprus, with Crete, and with the Hittite Empire (through the port of Ura).

Ugarit's access to the great maritime trading routes was vital to its success and prosperity, but these routes could only be exploited through the possession of a large merchant navy. The merchant fleet was composed of ships belonging to a variety of independent shipowners, though it is clear that the king himself was also engaged in merchant naval affairs. Some of the merchant ships were large by ancient standards. Although no ships are known to have survived in the vicinity of Ugarit, a number of anchors have been excavated, and from these it is possible to estimate the size of the ships. The anchors were made from stone, a custom which is still followed in certain small ports along the eastern Mediterranean seaboard; the stone was quarried locally,

FIGURE 11: Eastern Mediterranean: Overland and sea routes from Ugarit

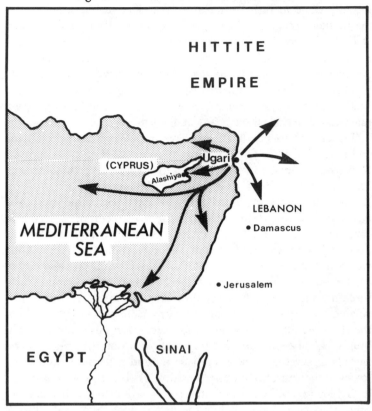

and the types employed included sandstone, limestone, basalt, and granite. Of the thirty or so anchors excavated in Ugarit and the nearby seaport, the four largest specimens weigh approximately half a ton each. Others range between 220 and 400 pounds. It has been estimated that a half-ton anchor would have been used on a ship weighing two hundred tons or more, with a length of about seventy feet. Freight on such ships, consisting of metal, grain, or other goods, could have weighted up to five hundred tons. From this data, it is clear that shipping would have been both cheaper and more efficient than donkey transportation. (It is interesting that about seventeen of the anchors found in Ugarit were excavated in the temple area, indicating that seagoing life had thoroughly penetrated the religious thought and activity of the citizens of Ugarit.) Some further information about shipping recently came to light as a result of underwater archaeology off the southern coast of Turkey. Archaeologists, diving off the shore at Cape Gelidonya, discovered the remains of a ship which sank there *circa* 1200 B.C. The ship was only about thirty feet long, but was carrying nearly one ton of copper ingots and about fifty pounds of tin. It had apparently been engaged in trade between southern Anatolia and ports on the eastern Mediterranean; the tin may have been taken on board at Ugarit.

Ugarit and its port may also have played a role in the buying and renting of ships for merchant purposes. One of the documents from the palace archives is a letter from an Egyptian official to Pharaoh Amenophis III; it concerns the desire of the king of Alashiya to buy some ships from an Egyptian shipowner. The transaction required the pharaoh's approval before it could be completed, and the official in Ugarit sought to persuade him to give such approval. At that time, a large amount of shipbuilding was being undertaken in Egypt, but it is possible that the city of Ugarit functioned as an outlet for Egyptian ships being sold to foreign nations. Another text describes the king of Ugarit borrowing, or leasing, a number of ships from the king of Byblos; the ships were to be used in some major mercantile venture. The king of Ugarit was required to pay the king of Byblos 540 silver shekels as surety for the loan or lease, and a further fifty shekels to cover the cost of outfitting the ships. If the ships were returned to Byblos in good condition, the surety would be returned to the king of Ugarit, less a fee for the use; in the event of the loss of the ships, however, the Ugaritic king would forfeit his deposit.

The movement of ships and donkeys in and out of Ugarit provided the foundation of wealth. Gold and ivory were imported from Egypt. Silver and tin were imported from the Hittite state in Anatolia. Copper was imported from Alashiya (Cyprus). Wood, copper, and various manufactured goods were exported to Egypt. Grain and gold were exported to the Hittite Empire. Locally manufactured textiles, oil, and wine were exported to a variety of destinations. This movement of goods through the kingdom, together with the various duties and taxes which that movement produced, became the basis of Ugarit's wealth.

The metal trade demonstrates more clearly than other aspects of commerce the potential which Ugarit's trading position provided. The money base in the ancient world of that time was silver, specifically the silver shekel (which was both a unit and a weight). Silver was mined principally in northeastern Anatolia, and the trade in silver was controlled initially by the Hittites. The value of other metals may be assessed on the basis of a shekel of silver. Some approximate equivalents are provided in the following table:

FIGURE 12: APPROXIMATE METAL PRICES IN UGARIT'S GOLDEN AGE

1 shekel silver = 227 shekels tin
1 shekel silver = 200 to 235 shekels copper
3 or 4 shekels silver = 1 shekel gold

Though silver was the base of the money system, gold was the more valuable commodity, approximately three or four times the value of silver. In Egypt, gold could be purchased relatively cheaply, for it was mined in southern Egypt and probably also in central Arabia. Thus Ugarit was able to make a considerable profit by importing relatively cheap gold from Egypt, which was then sold to the Hittites for a higher price, or exchanged for silver or other raw and manufactured goods. (Gold was not the most valuable commodity at the time. Iron, mined in northeastern Anatolia, was gradually coming into use during this period, but it was so costly [iron: silver = 1:40] that only the rich and royalty had access to it. There is no clear evidence regarding trade in iron at Ugarit.) Thus Ugarit, functioning as commercial middleman between Egypt and the Hittite Empire, was able to benefit from speculation on the gold and silver markets. In these and other metals, the kingdom of Ugarit during its Golden Age became the center of the ancient world's metal trade.

The wealth accumulated through trade was reflected in a high standard of living in the city of Ugarit. Not only were many houses of large size, but the objects found in them and in the royal palace indicate the possession of wealth by many of the citizens of Ugarit. Jewelry, gold objects, beautiful ceramic vessels, finely carved ivories, and other objets d'art are all indicative of a thriving and prosperous society. In gross terms, Ugarit was not the largest or wealthiest of the Near Eastern states; it could not compare with the enormous size and wealth of Egypt or the

Hittite Empire. But in a relative perspective, the small state was wealthy and cosmopolitan. Its wealth was accompanied by a rich culture, a flourishing of the arts, fine literature, and a mosaic of coexisting religions. It was a civilized and urbane city, which had few parallels in the ancient world. Yet its civilization was not to survive. The decline of Ugarit was entirely the result of external forces beyond its control; there is no evidence at all of an inner moral or social decline contributing to its demise.

It was the movement of the Sea Peoples throughout the eastern Mediterranean world towards the end of the thirteenth century B.C. which was to bring about the destruction of Ugarit. The term "Sea Peoples" is in some ways a misnomer, for it covers at least five groups of people who sometimes operated in concert; but some of them functioned mainly on the basis of naval power, while others possessed troops that operated primarily on the land. These peoples probably came originally from the vicinity of the Aegean and southeastern Europe; about midway through the thirteenth century, they began a massive and powerful military expansion eastwards into the Mediterranean world. They were responsible for the decline and fall of the Hittite Empire. They threatened Egypt and engaged with the Egyptians in both land and sea battles. Some of them, referred to in the Bible as Philistines, settled in Palestine (which is named after them) and for a while threatened the survival of the Hebrew immigrants there. And it was the Sea Peoples who devastated Ugarit.

The end probably came during the reign of Ammurapi (though there is some uncertainty with respect to the history of the last kings of Ugarit). Letters excavated at Ras Shamra, dated from the last days of Ugarit's existence, provide some insight into events. Both the Hittites and the king of Alashiya were desperately worried by the power of the invaders and sought Ugarit's aid. The Ugaritic navy was dispatched westwards to guard the entrance to the Mediterranean from the Aegean Sea. The army was sent north to help the Hittite army in its efforts to stall the overland assault. But both the navy and the army were defeated, and as a consequence the kingdom of Ugarit was left defenseless in the face of the advancing invaders. The city was easily conquered; some of its citizens fled to safety, but others were massacred by the conquerors. Many of the city's great buildings were burned to the ground. Others were simply abandoned and, since the inhabitants never returned, they fell gradually into a state of decay. The Sea Peoples apparently did not rebuild the city or attempt to maintain it; the inhabitants never returned. Ugarit had died! Nevertheless, the city has left a legacy for the modern world in the form of its literature.

Chapter IV:
UGARITIC LANGUAGE
AND LITERATURE

ALTHOUGH the physical remains of the ancient city of Ugarit
are of considerable significance, it is the written texts which have
a particular and distinctive importance. Without those texts, we
would have only a visual impression of the city, its layout, and
principal buildings; we would know a little of the style of life
from the surviving artifacts. But the past would remain essentially
a skeleton; it is the written texts that flesh out that skeleton, providing an insight into the names of persons, their daily lives and
business transactions, their religious beliefs, their hopes and fears,
and the multitude of other details which constitute the very fabric
of human history.

The written texts are important not only for the study of Ugarit's life and history; they are also vital for the comparative study
of the world of Ugarit and the Old Testament world. Their value
is increased by the relative lack of similar textual evidence from
the southern geographical region of Palestine in which the Hebrews settled early in the biblical period. From the historical
period of the Old Testament, very few ancient texts have been
recovered by archaeologists. Complete Hebrew inscriptions from
the early biblical period number less than twenty, and none of
them are long. To this evidence can be added that of approximately
150 seals, each containing no more than one or two words (usually
names). Several hundred jar-handle stamps have also survived,
but these too consist usually of only a very few words, again
usually personal names. The few surviving Hebrew inscriptions,
together with two Moabite inscriptions, constitute the principal
epigraphic evidence of a relatively early date that is relevant to the
study of the Old Testament. But, with the exception of the biblical
text itself, nothing has survived from the early period that could
be called literature in the proper sense.

To some extent, this absence of comparative textual material has been offset by the numerous texts recovered from various archives in Egypt (e.g., el-Amarna) and Mesopotamia (e.g., Mari). But while these resources are of considerable value for the comparative study of biblical texts, they are not of primary value. They are written, for the most part, in the Egyptian and Akkadian languages; Egyptian belongs to a different language family from Hebrew, while Akkadian (with its subgroups, Babylonian and Assyrian) is a Semitic language, but not a close linguistic relative of Hebrew. Furthermore, there are considerable cultural differences between the civilizations, and hence between the literatures of Egypt and Mesopotamia on the one hand and that of the Hebrews on the other hand. For these and other reasons, the value of the great mass of written texts from Egypt and Mesopotamia must be considered as secondary with respect to the comparative study of biblical Hebrew literature.

It is against this general background that the potential value of the Ugaritic texts may be seen. The archives of Ugarit contained texts in a variety of languages, but those in the Ugaritic language per se are of first importance, given the linguistic proximity of Ugaritic to Hebrew. The archives at Ras Shamra have yielded so far some fourteen hundred texts in the Ugaritic language. While some of these texts are fragmentary, and a small number are illegible, the majority constitute primary data for the comparative study of the Hebrew Bible. And while fourteen hundred texts in the Ugaritic language may not seem to be a large number when compared with the recent discoveries at Tell Mardikh in Syria (see further Chapter VI), it is nevertheless a very considerable body of data when compared with the slender textual resources in Hebrew language that have survived outside the biblical tradition itself.

The Ugaritic tablets from Ras Shamra are written in the alphabetic cuneiform script, deciphered through the efforts of Virolleaud, Bauer, and Dhorme. Though this cuneiform script is called alphabetic, it is not alphabetic in the modern and strict sense of that word; it is semisyllabic, and only one of the letters (in three different forms) gives any clue to the vowels, and hence the pronunciation, of Ugaritic words. Thus, to the modern eye, most Ugaritic words (when transliterated from cuneiform) look odd and unpronounceable (which they are, in the absence of a knowledge of the living language). To give some selected examples of Ugaritic words: *yd* = "hand"; *klb* = "dog"; *mlk* = "king"; *ndr* = "vow." Common words of this kind can be vocalized and pronounced on the basis of usage in other Semitic languages, though inevitably such a process of adding vowels that are not actually indicated in the writing system must be speculative and hypothetical.

The single consonant that is represented with vocalization is the letter that is called *aleph* in Hebrew, or *alif* in Arabic. It has no precise equivalent in the English alphabet; phonetically it may be described as a laryngal plosive (not unlike the sound of the English indefinite article "a"). It is represented in transliteration by the sign '. This letter has three forms in the cuneiform script, representing respectively: '*a*, '*i*, and '*u* (see further *Figure 13*). Hence, in those words which happen to contain the *aleph*, the script provides a partial clue as to their vocalization and pronunciation. Some examples are the following words: '*ab* = "father"; '*adm* = "mankind"; '*il* = "god"; *lb'u* = "lion"; *gr'a* = "he called."

The consequence of this limitation in the writing system is that a sentence in Ugaritic looks totally unspeakable, for its vowels (though known well enough by the persons who originally used the writing system) are not fully indicated. Consider the following Ugaritic sentence, together with its translation:

yš'u . gh . wyṣḥ . b'l . mt

"He raised (*yš'u*) his voice (*gh*) and shouted (*wyṣḥ*): Baal (*b'l*) is dead (*mt*)."

The sentence illustrates a further feature of the Ugaritic script, which it shares with scripts such as Arabic and Hebrew. Several of the consonants in the alphabet have no precise equivalents in the English alphabet and indeed represent sounds not normally employed in modern Western (Indo-European) languages. *Figure 13* lists the symbols of the Ugaritic alphabet, together with their corresponding letters, or an indication of their sound.

The absence of full vocalization probably created no difficulty for the average scribe or reader in ancient Ugarit, any more than the normally unvocalized modern Arabic or Hebrew script creates confusion for the readers of those scripts. Nevertheless, there are

FIGURE 13: The Ugaritic cuneiform alphabet

Sign	Equivalent	Sign	Equivalent
(cuneiform)	à	(cuneiform)	k
(cuneiform)	ì	(cuneiform)	l
(cuneiform)	ù	(cuneiform)	m
(cuneiform)	b	(cuneiform)	n
(cuneiform)	g	(cuneiform)	s
(cuneiform)	d	(cuneiform)	ṡ
(cuneiform)	ž	(cuneiform)	•
(cuneiform)	h	(cuneiform)	ġ
(cuneiform)	w	(cuneiform)	p
(cuneiform)	z	(cuneiform)	ṣ
(cuneiform)	ḥ	(cuneiform)	q
(cuneiform)	ḫ	(cuneiform)	r
(cuneiform)	ṭ	(cuneiform)	š
(cuneiform)	ẓ	(cuneiform)	t
(cuneiform)	y	(cuneiform)	ṯ

some difficulties for the modern reader of the ancient script, arising principally from lack of familiarity with the living language. A famous English phrase, presented without vocalization, illustrates the problem.

th ct n th mt

What does the phrase mean? What are the missing vowels? "The cat on the mat." Correct! But it could also be vocalized as (a) "the act on the mat," (b) "the coat in the moat," (c) "the cut in the meat"—and doubtless there are further variations. Usually, the context in which the phrase appeared would remove all ambiguities, as is normally the case with the Ugaritic texts. But in the reading of ancient texts, in which the meaning of all words is not known with certainty, it is inevitable that there are many ambiguities. Consequently, in most translations of the Ugaritic texts, there are always a number of uncertainties as to whether any particular translation is correct or precise.

The difficulties created by the absence of vocalization may be compounded by the actual condition of the text or the clay tablet. Many of the tablets are broken, leaving lines incomplete, stories unfinished, and accounts with no bottom line. In some cases, the tablet may be complete, but surface abrasions or the wear of time may have left the inscribed text essentially illegible (see *Figure 14*). These types of difficulties confound still further the efforts of scholars to provide clear and coherent translations. Most technical translators, sticking faithfully to the surviving evidence, fill their renditions with question marks, gaps, and the like; such translations make for frustrating, if accurate, reading! (The translated extracts from the texts provided later in this chapter have been "polished"; the gaps and problems in the original texts have been set aside in an attempt to provide clearly the sense of the quoted passages.)

The actual invention of the cuneiform alphabet remains to some extent shrouded in mystery. It is not the oldest known form of alphabetic writing, though it comes very close to deserving that honor. The oldest alphabet was no doubt the Canaanite linear alphabet, known from limited data such as the Byblos inscription and the so-called "Proto-Sinaitic Inscriptions" discovered at the ancient copper and turquoise mines in the Sinai Peninsula; the Canaanite linear alphabet may go back to the sixteenth century B.C. The cuneiform alphabet of Ugarit is known to have been in use by the mid-fourteenth century; some of the Ugaritic texts can be dated precisely to the reign of Niqmadu III, *circa* 1360. Indeed, it is probable that the common usage of the cuneiform alphabet in Ugarit was in the process of being established, or authorized, during Niqmadu's reign.

FIGURE 14: Clay tablet (Ras Shamra, 1929), indicating difficulties in reading (from surface abrasions)

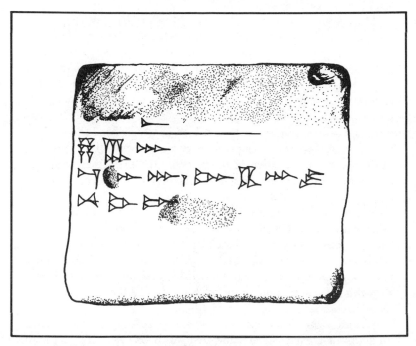

Not only is the date of the cuneiform alphabet's origin unknown, but the basis of its invention also remains unclear. It was probably devised by the scribes of Ugarit, who would have been trained (prior to the discovery of the cuneiform alphabet) in the Babylonian type of syllabic cuneiform writing. Having become familiar in their training with the principles of cuneiform writing, they would later have become acquainted with the simpler Canaanite linear script. The latter employed a set of signs to represent sounds (consonants), ignoring for practical purposes the vowels. The Ugaritic scribes adapted this principle to cuneiform, establishing twenty-seven symbols for the basic necessary consonants. The cuneiform symbols they devised do not appear to contain any visual significance; they were designed to be basically simple, and hence easy to write, and to be different from the symbols already employed in the Babylonian or Akkadian cuneiform. The original twenty-seven-letter alphabet was later expanded to a thirty-letter alphabet, with the introduction of, among other things, distinctive forms of the letter *aleph* to represent the three basic vowels that might accompany it.

The regular thirty-letter Ugaritic alphabet has been found in texts excavated at Ras Shamra, Minet el-Beida, Ras Ibn Hani (see Chapter VI), and by Danish excavators at Tell Sukas, some twenty miles south of Latakia. But a shorter form of the long alphabet, derived from it, has also been discovered in various excavations. A few texts in the short alphabet are known from Ras Shamra. Other examples come from Tell Nebi Mend, Kamid el-Loz, Sarepta, Beth-shemesh, Taanach, and the vicinity of Mt. Tabor. This wide distribution of the script, from Syria in the north to Palestine in the south, is indicative of the fact that the principles of alphabetic cuneiform writing became well-known and were employed on a fairly extensive basis.

The genius of the invention, in other words, lay in all probability with the scribes of ancient Ugarit. They are known to have been persons with extensive training and a knowledge of various languages and scripts. Quadrilingual texts found at Ras Shamra give some indication of their knowledge and breadth of training. Probably, at some date prior to 1400 B.C., the invention was made by the scribes.

Scribes were clearly persons of some standing in the ancient kingdom of Ugarit. Their education was broad, with respect both to languages and to the variety of writing systems current at that time. (A modern parallel would be a person familiar with the languages and scripts of Arabic, Russian, and Chinese, in addition to English.) Thus the scribes were not the ancient equivalents of the modern stenographer. On the other hand, the scribes were not necessarily artists or authors in any conventional sense. For example, it is known that many of the key mythological texts, some of which have considerable literary value, were written down *circa* 1360 by a distinguished scribe called *'Ilmlk* (probably "Ilmilku"). But it is unlikely that he was the author of these texts; either he recorded on clay the older oral traditions, or he copied out (and perhaps edited) older written traditions. If the older written records were in another script, he may have adapted them to the new alphabetic script.

A little is known of the education of the scribes from the abecedaries and school texts recovered in the excavations at Ras Shamra.

Many of these short texts contain simply the letters of the alphabet, written down one by one in an unexperienced hand. Sometimes a group of letters are repeated over and over again, the errors in the initial attempts eventually being eliminated as the exercise progressed. Other school texts contain the same word written over and over again, in the search for perfection, and more advanced exercises reveal the student copying out an epistle, to learn the more advanced elements of the scribal arts.

The Ugaritic language, which was preserved in the cuneiform alphabet, has already been described as a close linguistic relative of Biblical Hebrew: both are Semitic languages. The Semitic family of languages is generally subdivided into three main groups. The East Semitic languages were used for the most part in Mesopotamia and comprise principally the dialects of Akkadian, namely Assyrian and Babylonian. The South Semitic languages include Classical Arabic, Old South Arabian, and Ethiopic. The third subgroup is conventionally labelled Northwest Semitic; this group includes both Ugaritic and Hebrew, together with various other languages and dialects (e.g., Phoenician, Moabite, and various other Canaanite dialects). The precise linguistic relationship between Ugaritic and Hebrew remains a matter of debate among scholars. Some view the two languages as being closely related, essentially regional dialects of a general Canaanite language within the Northwest Semitic group. Others consider the two to be less intimately related, emphasizing the differences between them rather than the similarities. The very nature of the surviving evidence is such that a firm conclusion to the debate may never be possible.

Nevertheless, it is clear that the two languages have a great deal in common. They share many common words, which, though they may have been pronounced differently, clearly have the same meaning (see *Figure 15*). The grammatical structures of two languages share many common features. And even in the matter of literary conventions, the two languages display a considerable degree of overlap. Thus, although the precise linguistic relationship between Ugaritic and Hebrew cannot be settled beyond dispute, the degree of commonality is sufficiently large to form the basis of the extensive comparative studies of Ugaritic and Hebrew language and literature that have been undertaken during the last half century.

The Ugaritic clay tablets were found in various different ar-

FIGURE 15: Examples of common Ugaritic-Hebrew words
(Hebrew words are given without Masoretic
vocalization)

UGARITIC	HEBREW	MEANING
mlk	*mlk*	king
bt	*byt*	house
ks	*kws*	cup
lšn	*lšwn*	tongue
ṣdq	*ṣdq*	righteous
gdl	*gdwl*	large
yd	*yd*	hand
hkl	*hykl*	palace
ḥlb	*ḥlb*	milk
ymn	*ymyn*	right hand
'pr	*'pr*	dust
lb	*lb*	heart

chives and libraries throughout the remains of the ancient city, and though the location of each find is important for the interpretation of any particular text, the archives as such contained a varied assortment of texts. In the large palace, some five separate archives have been found at different locations within the massive structure. These were archives in the proper sense, or repositories; in general, they contained texts of an economic or administrative character, in various languages and scripts, that were stored as records, for the usual administrative reasons. In one area of the palace, an oven was found in which soft clay tablets were being baked to the hardness that would make them durable; apparently the palace was destroyed while the tablets were still in the oven. The tablets in question included administrative and mythological texts, but also some epistles which provide insight into the state of affairs in the kingdom of Ugarit during the very last days and hours of its existence. The smaller palace, adjacent to the large palace, also had an archive, containing principally administrative texts written in Babylonian cuneiform.

The principal religious and mythological texts come from two priestly libraries, though a few mythological texts and fragments were also found in the more secular archives. The library in the high priest's house, which may have functioned as a priestly or scribal school, contained the principal mythological and legendary tablets (described later in this chapter). A little to the south of this library was the house of the so-called "priest magician." Its library contained not only portions of mythological texts, but also terracotta models of lungs and livers, on which were inscriptions; these lung and liver models were used in the ancient practice of divination.

Two private libraries have also been excavated. One of these libraries, with very diverse contents, was found in the large house of Rapanou (see Chapter III). Rapanou's library included various texts of a scientific nature, written in Akkadian; a quadrilingual lexicon containing words in Ugaritic, Babylonian, Sumerian, and Hurrian; a magical text; and various letters of a diplomatic nature. Another private citizen's library, in a house situated to the south of the acropolis area, contained amongst other texts a fragment of the famous Babylonian Flood Story, known more completely from texts found in the Mesopotamian region.

It is the combined resources of these libraries and archives that have provided the extant corpus of Ugaritic texts. As should be clear already, few of the surviving Ugaritic texts deserve the title "literature," in the strict sense. The great majority of the texts are relatively short and of an administrative or economic nature. They are vital for the reconstruction of Ugarit's civilization and history, but less valuable in providing information about the literature and religion of ancient Ugarit. For this kind of information, we must turn to those tablets containing legends and myths, which are at once literary in form and, to judge by the principal location in which they were discovered, religious in function.

The literary texts from Ugarit are almost entirely in the form of poetry (excluding, for practical purposes, epistles from the category of literature), and it is with respect to the conventions of Ugaritic poetry that there can be discerned one of the principal areas of similarity to the biblical literature. As a general statement, it is fair to say that Hebrew and Ugaritic poets employed the same basic conventions and structures.

The most distinctive form of Ugaritic poetry is what is called parallelism, a form familiar from its frequent usage in biblical

poetry. The units of parallelistic poetry consist normally of two
or three lines, in which the first line expresses the basic thought,
which is then elaborated in the following lines. In synonymous parallelism, the essential thought of the first line is repeated in the
second (and sometimes in the third) line, commonly by the use
of synonyms, or near synonyms, and sometimes by way of direct
repetition. The following two lines from the Baal myth illustrate
the standard form of synonymous parallelism, the second line
essentially repeating the essence of the first.

> The gods also sat down to eat,
>   the sons of the Holy One to dine.

The "gods" are the same as the "sons of the Holy One"; the verb
"to eat" in the first line is balanced by "to dine" in the second line.
Another example from the same text illustrates the principle further, this time in a three-line poetic unit.

> Now your adversaries, O Baal;
>   now you must smite your adversaries,
>   now you must silence your enemies.

The second example makes it clear that parallelism is not merely
a mechanical device; within its general limitations, immense variety is possible, and though sometimes parallelistic poetry may
be tedious to read, it may also be surprising and stimulating in
its turn of phrase and development of thought.

Much of Ugaritic poetry is more impressive for its epic and
narrative force than for the sheer literary beauty of its lines and
words; but sometimes the Ugaritic poets achieved poetry that is
remarkable in its own right. The following quotation, from a
portion of the Baal myth, is provided in two languages and illustrates the potential power of the Ugaritic poets. The Ugaritic text
is given first, simply to provide some indication of the sound and
the line length.

> *dm . rgm . iṯ . ly . w. 'argmk*
> *hwt . w. 'aṯnyk*
> *rgm . 'ṣ . w . lḫšt . 'abn*
> *t'ant . šmm . 'm . 'arṣ*
> *thmt . 'mn . kbkbm*

54

'abn . brq . dl . td' . šmm
rgm . ltd' . nšm
wltbn . hmlt . 'arṣ

I have a tale I would tell you,
   a report I would repeat to you;
a tale of woodland
   and a whisper of stone,
a sighing of heavens to earth,
   of ocean deeps to stars:
"I create lightning not comprehended by heavens,
   the tale not known by humans,
   not understood by earth's multitudes."

This passage, in striking language, describes the essential power of the storm-god Baal, a power contained within the mysterious force of lightning, which somehow links the heavens and the earth together.

We must now turn to the principal literary texts from ancient Ugarit and provide some description of them, together with the essence of the narratives and some examples of their literary form and style. In the first example, the Legend of King Keret, some detail of the story and poetry will be given to convey the flavor of Ugaritic literature. More summary accounts will be provided for other Ugaritic literary texts.

1. The Legend of King Keret

The ancient legend of Keret was recorded on three clay tablets, all of a fairly large size, with the writing in three vertical columns on each side of the tablets. The tablets were discovered during the second and third campaigns at Ras Shamra during 1930 and 1931; they were a part of the high priest's library collection discovered near the two temples situated in the northern part of the city. All three tablets are now preserved in the Syrian National Museum at Aleppo. They are identified as the work of the well-known scribe, Ilmilku.

The condition in which the tablets have survived gives a good indication of the kind of difficulties facing any translator and interpreter of the Ugaritic texts. The first of the three tablets, though it had been broken (and subsequently restored), is in relatively good condition; it is easily legible and about seventy-five percent complete. The second tablet in the sequence has fared less well; it was badly broken at some point in the past and the two surviving portions are very limited in scope. The third tablet was also broken, but the three remaining pieces have been put together, leaving a little more than half of the original text in a fairly clear and legible form. Thus, the complete story of Keret is not fully known (though it was probably contained in its entirety on the three surviving tablets; there appear to be no missing tablets); nevertheless, enough has survived to provide an outline of the legend as a whole.

The story concerns a king who was already regarded a figure from antiquity in the time of the kingdom of Ugarit; his name was *KRT*, usually vocalized as Keret, though it is rendered Kirta in some translations. The story begins with a description of the terrible plight in which King Keret found himself. As a consequence of various disasters, almost all of his family had been destroyed. And worse still, though he had had seven wives, each had died from some misfortune, leaving the king without progeny or an heir to the throne. Devastated by disaster, the king went weeping to his room; but when sleep eventually overpowered him, he had a dream.

As he wept, he fell asleep;
　　as his tears flowed, he slumbered.
Sleep overwhelmed him as he lay down;
　　slumber overpowered him as he curled up.
Then, in his dream, El came down;
　　in his vision, there was the Father of Humans!
And drawing near, he asked Keret:
　　"Why is it that Keret weeps?
Why does El's favorite son shed tears?"

Keret responds to the supreme god, El, by indicating his desire for sons and an heir. And so he is ordered to offer sacrifices, both to El and to the god Baal, after which he is to prepare a great army and set out on a military campaign for the state of Udm, ruled over by King Pabil. The purpose of the campaign is not simply to secure booty and victory, but to demand that Pabil's beautiful daughter, Huray, be given to King Keret in marriage. On waking from his sleep, Keret puts into action the instructions he had received from the god El and sets out for Udm with a massive army. On the third day of the expedition, the king comes to a sacred shrine of the goddess Athirat; there he makes a vow that if he obtains the princess Huray he will donate great sums of silver and gold to the goddess. Then he continues on his journey, and after four more days of travel his army pitches camp before Udm. King Pabil sends messengers who offer Keret various gifts, but he refuses them all, insisting that he desires only the princess, Huray.

"Give me Princess Huray,
    the most beautiful of your family, your first born,
whose beauty is like that of Anat,
    whose fairness like that of Athirat,
whose eyes are precious gems,
    whose eyelids bowls of onyx."

After some demur, the princess is given to King Keret, who then returns to his own land. In the years that follow, Keret and Huray become the parents of many sons and daughters.

Years later, misfortune again strikes King Keret, this time in the form of a grave illness. The story is less clear at this point, for the text is broken and incomplete, but it seems that the sickness of Keret is prolonged and affects the health and stability of his kingdom. The rains are curtailed, the crops reduced, and violent men have grown strong in the exploitation of the weak and the powerless. But the supreme god El enters the story again and seeks a god from among the members of the divine assembly who would be able to heal Keret from his sickness. When none is to be found, El creates a female spirit, whom he sends to Keret with instructions to heal him. The spirit, Sha'taqat, went to Keret and, touching him with a magic wand, healed him of his sickness, and then the failing king's zest returned.

His throat opened for food,
    his mouth for a meal!
Death was defeated,
    Sha'taqat was totally victorious!
Then the noble King Keret issued orders,
    raising his voice and shouting:
"Listen to this, Princess Huray:
slaughter a sheep and I'll eat it,
    and a calf, too — I'll devour it."

After eating, Keret's strength returned and he sat once again on his throne, fully in control of his royal powers. But his son Yassib, thinking perhaps that his father was still sick and not in control of his powers, had hatched a plot to take over the kingdom. Yassib approached the king and boldly declared the king's failings, which had been a consequence of sickness. But he had badly underestimated his father's renewed vitality, and the story, which began with Keret desperate for a male heir, concludes with the same king declaring a curse on his over-ambitious son, Yassib.

"My son:
may the god Horon smash your head,
    Athtart-Name-of-Baal smash your forehead.
May you fall at the boundary of your years
    with empty hands, and be humbled."

The precise significance of the legend is a matter of continuing debate, though first and foremost it was a story and of literary value. But its themes were significant in the ancient world, focusing as they did on the ideological dimensions of kingship. The king, called the "son of god" (El), was responsible to his god for the control of human society, and for the protection of orphans and those in need of aid. The king who had no heir, had no long-term security in his reign, inviting others to squabble over the succession. The king who was sick could not carry out fully his royal duties in the control of his kingdom. And the king who did not control firmly any overtly ambitious children could lose his control of the kingdom as a whole. Thus, in a variety of ways, the story develops the ideals of kingship in the ancient world, and indicates the directions from which a good and stable monarchy might be threatened.

2. The Legend of Aqhat

As was the case with the story of Keret, the Legend of Aqhat is preserved on three clay tablets, two reasonably well preserved, the third (or second, in the sequence of the story) in very bad condition. But whereas the story of Keret is reasonably clear from the extant evidence, that of Aqhat breaks off shortly before it reaches it climax. The reader is left in suspense, not knowing the end of the story, which will never be told unless the last missing fragment of the final tablet is discovered. All three surviving tablets were recovered during the second campaign at Ras Shamra in 1930, and all were recorded by the scribe Ilmilku and lodged in the high priest's library.

The story begins with a description of Daniel (also rendered Dan'el), perhaps a king, but more likely a patriarchal chieftain akin to Abraham. And, like both Keret and Abraham, Daniel had no son, but desired one, both to take care of him when old age came and to continue the family line after the patriarch's death. In response to prayer, the supreme god El decrees that Daniel shall have a son. On hearing the divine promise, Daniel is delighted and eagerly awaits the passing of the months until his son will be born.

The lad Aqhat is born without incident and grows up to be a dutiful son. One day, the king is visited by the craftsman of the gods, called Kothar-w-Ḥasis, who has fashioned a special bow and arrows. The divine craftsman gives the bow to Daniel, who in turn presents it to his son Aqhat. But the bow marks the beginning of trouble. The goddess Anat, mistress of love and war, sees the marvelous bow and wants it for herself. She offers to purchase it from Aqhat.

"Listen, I pray, O hero Aqhat.
Ask for silver! I will give you it.
Gold! I will grant it to you,
     but give your bow to Anat."

When Aqhat refuses silver and gold, Anat promises to give him even more marvellous gifts.

"Ask for life, O hero Aqhat!
     Ask for life — I will give it to you!
     Eternal life — I will grant it to you!"

But the young man perceives that the beautiful goddess is offering what she cannot deliver and scathingly rejects her.

"Do not lie, lady,
     for to a hero, your lying is rubbish.
What does a human finally get?
     What is a human's ultimate fate?
Plaster will be poured on my head,
     lime on my forehead,
and I shall die the common death
     —yes, I shall indeed die!"

But Aqhat, in refusing the violent goddess, has encountered a dangerous foe, and Anat calls upon the services of her henchman Yatpan to murder the hero of the story. Disguised as a bird, Yatpan attacks Aqhat during a meal and kills him. But the consequences of the hero's death are disastrous; the rains are withheld and the crops fail. Pughat, the hero's sister, does not know of her brother's death, but perceiving the drought and the hovering eagles in the sky, she concludes that a murder has been committed. She communicates her suspicions to Daniel, who then travels around his territory to locate the source of the trouble. And then he learns of the death of his son and vows vengeance on the murderer, whose identity is still unknown to him; the remains of Aqhat, found in the belly of an eagle, are buried in the family grave.

It is the daughter Pughat who investigates and discovers that Yatpan was instrumental in her brother's death; she then assumes the responsibility for avenging her dead brother. With vengeance in her heart and a sword hidden within her flowing robes, Pughat disguises herself as Anat and pays a visit to Yatpan. She is welcomed by the villain, who thinks her to be his mistress and invites her into his house for a drink. And as Yatpan joins his guest in drinking, his tongue is loosened with liquor and he boasts of his violent deeds on behalf of Anat.

"The hand that slaughtered the hero Aqhat
    shall slay thousands of my Lady's enemies!"

But just as the unknowing confession falls from Yatpan's lips and Pughat's vengeance is expected, the clay tablet is broken and the end of the story is lost.

The incompleteness of the story has naturally contributed uncertainty as to its meaning and interpretation. It seems to be set in a more distant, patriarchal world than is the legend of Keret; humans and divine beings freely intermix in the course of daily life. But many of the themes are familiar from other Near Eastern literature: the concern for a son and successor, the fertility of the land, blood vengeance for an act of murder, and conflict with the goddess of love and war. Given the incompleteness of the text, a precise interpretation may never be possible, but enough of the story has survived to indicate one basic reason for its preservation in ancient times; a good story, well told, retains its fascination from one generation to the next.

3. The Mythology of the God Baal

In the two literary texts summarized above, it is clear that El was the supreme god; but the content of both texts is much older than the Golden Age of Ugarit. And though the god El remained a significant deity in Ugarit's pantheon, in the Golden Age it was Baal, and perhaps also Dagan, who were the principal deities. The two excavated temples, situated close to each other in the northern sector of the city, are identified with the worship of Baal and Dagan (though the actual evidence for this association is far from certain). Dagan has a temple, but does not figure prominently in the literary texts; Baal, on the other hand, not only has a temple, but is a key figure in the fairly extensive collection of religious and literary texts found in the high priest's library. And the centrality of Baal is to be expected, in part because of the prominence of forms of the Baal religion throughout the Canaanite world. But as the god who controlled storm, lightning, and rain, he had a higher status than other gods of fertility. The fertility of the land, and hence its ability to produce crops and support cattle, depended ultimately upon Baal and his female partner Anat (who is sometimes described as his wife and sometimes as his sister). Thus, so far as can be determined, it was probably Baal, among the multitude of Ugarit's gods, who was the central focus of religious activity and human worship.

From the high priest's library came a number of texts containing the fundamental elements of the mythology of Baal. The primary information comes from a set of six clay tablets recovered during the second and third campaigns during 1930 and 1931. The tablets may well have formed a set, a "six-volume" literary work, and all the tablets appear to have been produced by the single, famous scribe, Ilmilku. The majority of the tablets contained six columns of writing, three columns on each side of the tablet, providing space on each tablet for a considerable quantity of text. But none of the tablets has survived in perfect condition. One is about seventy-five percent complete, two about fifty percent complete, and the three remaining tablets have survived with much less than half of their original content. Consequently, of the six-tablet sequence that constitutes the Baal cycle, only about half of the entire text is known. And it is important to note that very often the missing or illegible portions of the tablets are precisely those parts that are critical for the interpretation and understanding of the myth as a whole.

For example, the Baal tablets contain accounts of three key incidents in the mythology; but the broken and incomplete nature of the tablets is such that many key points of interpretation remain obscure. Thus, there is no certainty as to whether the three "stories of Baal" (summarized below) are all parts of one long story about Baal, or whether they are three quite independent stories. The six tablets may contain a single major story of Baal, or they may comprise an anthology of Baal stories from different places and different periods. And even if it were conceded that the tablets contained a single Baal story, of which the three surviving incidents were a part, there would still be considerable uncertainty as to the sequence in which the incidents should be read. And the sequence of events, in mythological narrative, can often be of considerable importance. The summaries of the three key incidents in the Baal story that follow are given in their probable sequence, if it may be granted that they belong to a single narrative!

(a) Baal and Yamm. The first narrative concerns the relations between Baal and the god Yamm, whose name means "Sea" (he is also called Nahar, or "River"); central to this part of the story is the conflict between Baal and Yamm. It is worth noting that the conflict account bears striking similarities to a portion of the Babylonian Creation Story, Enuma Elish ("When on High"), with its account of conflict between Tiamat ("Ocean Depths") and Marduk; the Babylonian and Ugaritic myths share, in all probability, some common heritage.

The opening scene, set in the divine world, indicates that El is the supreme god, but in practical matters he is not the supremely active god. The rising power in this divine world is the god Yamm, symbolizing the chaos and force of the ocean; he desires a palace to be built for him, which will both represent and establish his authority. Tension develops between Baal and Yamm, leading eventually to a battle between them. They begin to fight, and at first it seems that Yamm will be victorious; but Baal, who has been equipped by the divine craftsman with two special weapons, is ultimately victorious.

> Then the club danced from Baal's hand,
>> speeding like an eagle from his fingers.
> It caught Prince Yamm on the forehead —
>> right between the eyes of the Honorable Nahar!
> Yamm collapsed,
>> falling to the ground,
> his joints trembling,
>> his body crumpled.
> Baal dragged him out and set him down
>> and finished off the Honorable Nahar!

The end of the narrative is partially lost in broken text, but it is clear that Baal's victory was highly significant with respect to his status among the gods.

> Yamm is dead!
> Baal shall certainly become king.

The story, in outline form, is typical of one part of common Near Eastern creation myths. First, in the cosmogonic process, there are the gods of the primeval, chaotic waters; second, there come those gods who represent the ordered aspects of the emerging world. Then there emerges the classical tension between the powers of chaos and the forces of order, and only when order has triumphed over chaos can creation be said to be fully established. In this story, it is Yamm who represents the primeval forces of chaos and who threatens the emerging order of the world; Baal, representing fertility, is the heroic protagonist of order. And, in mythological terms, it is Baal's victory over Yamm that symbolizes the conquest of chaos by order. In this sense, the first part of the story has overtones of creation mythology; it is not a complete creation story, but it is typical of one classical portion of creation mythology. But apart from creation, the tension between order and chaos is always present in the world of nature, and the narrative of Baal's victory may also be perceived as an affirmation of the continuing triumph of order over chaos, which from a certain perspective was not merely an affirmation of the Baal religion, but also its principal goal.

(b) Baal's Palace. The second narrative in the myth is a long and complex account which culminates in the building of a palace for Baal. Yamm, in the opening story, had desired a palace, but his defeat at the hands of Baal had demolished his authority. Baal's victory established his kingship over the gods (under the ultimate supremacy of El), but a king without a palace was no king at all; hence the palace narrative develops the story of Baal from the point at which he earns the right to be king, by conquering Yamm, to the regular establishment of that right in the construction of a palace.

Again, the interrelationship between mythology and religion is evident in the palace episode. Baal's palace in the heavens was represented physically by his temple on earth. And the establishment of the heavenly palace is in some sense the foundational authority for the earthly temple. The two are vital for religion. The heavenly palace provided Baal with both authority and protection; so long as it survived, Baal would provide the earth with the beneficent rains so necessary for the crops. And the role of religion, in Baal's earthly temple, was the recognition of Baal's kingship and authority, and the attempt to secure it permanently against the ever threatening forces of chaos, whose return could culminate in drought and starvation.

The focal point of religion can thus be understood in terms of the chaos-order theme. The reality of the natural world is that the elements of both chaos and order are ever present, but in varying degrees. The orderly rains and seasons make provision for human life and survival, but the chaotic oceans and summer droughts, if they triumph over the orderly world, threaten the end to human life. Religious activity is not only an affirmation and belief in the triumph of order over chaos, but is also an attempt to secure the continuity of that triumph by means of regular worship, rituals, and sacrifice. Yet Yamm was only one of the gods representing chaos; the other principal power of chaos was the god Mot, who is the central figure in the third episode of the myth.

(c) Baal and Mot. In the story of Baal and Mot, it is the theme of conflict which is central once again. Mot, whose name means "Death," rises as a new threat to the power and authority of Baal, and the tension results eventually in two battles between them. In the first confrontation, Baal is defeated and is confined within the

netherworld ruled over by Mot. But eventually Baal is rescued by the combined efforts of two goddesses, Anat and Shapsh (the sun-goddess, an orderly deity). The violent goddess Anat achieves her deliverance by engaging Mot in conflict and slaying him.

> She grasped mighty Mot!
> She split him with a sword,
>   winnowed him with a sieve,
> burnt him with a fire,
>   and ground him with millstones;
> she scattered him in a field
>   for birds to eat his flesh
>   and sparrows to chew his limbs.
> Flesh cried out for flesh!

Baal returned to his earthly throne and authority, his chaotic enemy supposedly conquered. But making Death die is analogous to making water wet, and soon Mot reappears, "alive" again, still threatening the authority of Baal. On this occasion, Mot leaves his subterranean home and confronts Baal face to face in his mountain abode. Again, violent conflict breaks out.

> Mot is strong, Baal is strong!
>   They gore each other like buffaloes.
> Mot is strong, Baal is strong!
>   They bite each other like snakes.
> Mot is strong, Baal is strong!
>   They tug at each other like dogs.
> Mot is down, Baal is down on top of him!

The battle seems to end in a stalemate, and the situation is finally resolved only by the intervention of the supreme god El, who persuades Mot to return to his own domain and to allow Baal to resume his kingship. Death was not finally conquered, though the reign of order continued.

The most probable general interpretation of the six tablets concerning Baal is that they represent a compilation and standardization of a variety of stories about Baal. Ilmilku, who was responsible for the compilation, doubtless was also engaged in an editorial process, for the stories about Baal, though probably independent of each other originally, now have some narrative links to draw them together, sometimes in a rather artificial manner. What Ilmilku's purpose was in compiling this corpus of Baal texts remains uncertain. He may have been compiling an authoritative tradition, which eliminated at the same time minor and regional traditions about Baal. He may have been establishing a "Canaanite Bible," as an European scholar proposed a number of years ago. But in all probability, the cycle of mythological texts may have been utilized in some fashion within the worship of Baal's temple. Just what the relationship between the myth and the temple ritual might have been remains unknown, for the texts, as they have survived, do not contain the typical rubrics and notes that normally characterize ritual texts. Perhaps the great myths of Baal were read aloud in the temple of Baal during the seasonal festivals, for though they are literary in form, they were certainly designed for public reading and recitation.

This collection of texts pertaining to the god Baal is of considerable significance beyond the confines of the literature and civilization of Ugarit. Baal is known to have been worshipped in Egypt, Palestine, Syria, and in various parts of Mesopotamia. But prior to the discovery of the Ugaritic texts, few details were known about the nature of the belief in Baal. The Ugaritic texts have filled that gap. And the filling of the gap, as will become clear in the chapter that follows, is also of considerable significance for the study of the Old Testament and its world.

Chapter V:
THE OLD TESTAMENT AND UGARITIC STUDIES

A little more than fifty years ago, the kingdom of Ugarit was unknown; today, after nearly half a century of archaeological activity, it is well known. But the knowledge gained about that ancient city has had ramifications far beyond the boundaries of the small kingdom; it has revolutionized our knowledge of the biblical world. The civilization of Ugarit belongs to the general category of Canaanite civilization, which in turn is the immediate milieu for a large portion of the biblical narrative. And so a general knowledge of life as it used to be in Ugarit contributes to our capacity to understand the Old Testament world. Ugaritic studies elucidate not only the civilization of the neighbors of the Hebrews in ancient times, but also many of the customs and practices within Hebrew society as such. Consequently, one of the principal benefits of a knowledge of life in ancient Ugarit cannot easily be focused; it is simply the case that the knowledge helps one in general to understand the Old Testament world better, and to enter more fully into its life and culture.

Nevertheless, in the years since Ugarit's rediscovery, a great deal of detailed comparative work has been undertaken. Particular Ugaritic texts have been compared to particular Hebrew texts, and conclusions have been drawn. A religious custom reflected in Ugaritic literature has been compared to similar customs referred to in the biblical narrative. Proposals as to the correct meaning of obscure Hebrew words have been ventured on the basis of the meaning of cognate Ugaritic terms. In a variety of ways, precise hypotheses have been elaborated on the basis of comparative Ugaritic-Hebrew studies.

The comparative study of Ugarit and Israel is not without difficulties. Despite the similarity between Ugaritic civilization and Canaanite civilization, there are a number of differences, and so it cannot always be assumed that evidence drawn from Ugaritic sources will be truly representative of the Canaanite culture that flourished in the geographical region of Palestine to the south, where the main biblical events took place. And the geographical distance between Ugarit in the north and the biblical world in the south cannot be ignored; even today, in an age of mass communications, there are distinct differences between the Arabic spoken in Latakia (near Ras Shamra) and the Palestinian dialect in the south. Furthermore, the kingdom of Ugarit had flourished and declined before the Hebrew kingdoms had even entered the stage of history; consequently, there are serious difficulties of a chronological nature pertaining to all precise comparative studies. And a final problem relates to the nature of the data for comparative studies. The Ugaritic texts are often incomplete, semilegible, and difficult to interpret; the biblical texts have only survived after centuries of being copied and recopied by scribes.

Because of difficulties of this sort, the growth of comparative Ugaritic-Hebrew studies has been marked by both glorious triumphs and fearful errors. The difficulty one faces in reading the plethora of literature on the subject lies in distinguishing the triumphs from the tragedies! In the illustrations that follow, examples of both kinds are given. Some examples show the new and genuine understanding that Ugaritic studies have contributed to knowledge of the Old Testament. Others illustrate not only the dangers of comparative studies, but also how the promise of illumination may quickly fade when all the evidence is carefully examined.

The following illustrations of Ugarit's light on the Old Testament have been selected to demonstrate the varieties of kinds of illumination that may be shed on the biblical text. Some pertain to language and literature; others pertain to religion, culture, and civilization. But it should be stressed that the examples are merely samples; the actual wealth of ancient Ugarit for Old Testament studies is vastly greater than can be incorporated in these few pages.

1. Psalm 29 and the Canaanite Hymnbook

Writers are also readers and listeners. Consequently, the words a person writes may well be influenced by the words a person reads and hears. One part of the task of literary critics is to attempt to determine the words or works that may have influenced a writer in his art. Literary criticism has revealed that great and creative writers have been influenced in this way; the influence of Shakespeare can be seen in the writings of Byron or Shelley, or the influence of Milton in the lines of Wordsworth. One might expect that a similar kind of influence was exerted upon the biblical writers. Their insight and writings are distinctively their own, but external influences may have contributed to the particular formation and style of their writings.

In the early part of the twentieth century biblical scholars sought to delineate Egyptian and Babylonian influences upon the biblical writers. It was a natural tendency, for the extraordinary discoveries of the ancient civilizations of Babylon and Egypt opened up their literature to modern examination. But as is often the case in the world of scholarship, enthusiasm in comparisons led to speculation and dubious results. Some of the articles written in the earlier decades of this century would indicate, if taken literally, that the biblical writers had never entertained an original thought in their lives. Practically everything they wrote, it was suggested, was borrowed in its totality from the ancient Egyptians or Babylonians.

The discovery of Ras Shamra and Ugaritic literature made it a more natural process to turn to that literature in search of external influences upon biblical writers. Ugarit was closer to Israel than Babylon, and its language was a near relative of Hebrew. Thus, it could be speculated that an Israelite writer or composer might have read or heard the classics of Ugarit, or other works similar to them, and that such classics may have exerted an influence on him.

Psalm 29 provides a fascinating example of the evidence employed by scholars in their attempt to discern Canaanite or Ugaritic influence on the biblical poets. The psalm is a remarkably powerful hymn, employing the description of an awesome thunderstorm to evoke praise for the greatness and might of God. Thunder, described as the voice of God, is referred to seven times in the psalm; this magnificent voice, shaking the world of creation to its foundations, evokes the awe of worshippers. What external influences, if any, had been at work on the mind of the composer of this remarkable hymn?

In 1935 Harold L. Ginsberg, a distinguished Jewish scholar, put forward the hypothesis that Psalm 29 was originally a Phoenician hymn which had found its way into the biblical book of Psalms. Ginsberg's hypothesis immediately attracted the attention of responsible scholars, for he was thoroughly competent in Hebrew and a pioneer of Ugaritic studies; he was not a man given to rash hypotheses. In support of his argument Ginsberg pointed to "pagan notions" in the psalm, particularly to the emphasis throughout the psalm on the voice of the Lord; this emphasis, he suggested, indicated that the original version had been composed in honor of the Canaanite storm god, Baal. But there were also other distinctive features of Psalm 29. Geographical references in the psalm suggested a Phoenician or Syrian origin, and some grammatical peculiarities in its language pointed to a northern setting. Finally, the hymn closed with words reminiscent of the formula employed in the praise of Baal (Psalm 29:10), words known from the Ugaritic mythological texts.

Ginsberg's hypothesis was developed further by other scholars in the years that followed. Theodor H. Gaster suggested that Psalm 29 was originally a Canaanite psalm which had been "Yahwized"; that is, the name of Baal had been removed from the original and the personal name of the biblical God, Yahweh, had been inserted in its place. Gaster drew on analogy between this process and that employed in the early days of the Salvation Army, when secular songs were transformed into sacred hymns. As General William Booth, founder of the Salvation Army, is reputed to have said: "Why should the devil have all the best tunes?"

By 1950, the hypothesis seemed secure. Frank M. Cross, Jr., now at Harvard University, considered the evidence to be conclusive and therefore affirmed that Psalm 29 was a classic text for examining the nature of *Canaanite* poetry! Studies after 1950 turned to a new problem. If Psalm 29 really was Canaanite in its original form, what was it doing in the Bible? F. Charles Fensham, a South African scholar, suggested that the Hebrews may have used this hymn as part of a missionary effort; by using the psalm, zealous Israelites may have sought to reach the Canaanites and even those other Israelites who had fallen away from the true faith.

As one reflects on more than forty-five years of study concentrated on Psalm 29, a clearer picture begins to emerge. It is not really certain that Psalm 29 was taken over, lock, stock, and barrel, from Phoenicians or Canaanites, and merely "Yahwized." The evidence, under close examination, is rather too slender to support such a view. On the other hand, it does seem to have been established beyond reasonable doubt that Canaanite poetry has exerted some kind of influence on the writer or composer of Psalm 29. It is possible that the Hebrew poet found a Canaanite hymn which deeply impressed him and that then he modified it slightly to express more clearly his own understanding and praise of the God of the Hebrews. But it is perhaps more likely that the psalmist engaged in deliberate imitation for religious purposes. He desired to convey to his audience, or to the worshippers who would employ his psalm, the greatness of his God. But he wanted to make a theological point as well. God was not only the Lord of history, the One who had led his chosen people out of Egypt, on to Sinai, and then through the wilderness to the promised land. God was also the Lord of nature. The predecessors of Israel in the promised land, the Canaanites, had believed Baal to be the lord of nature. The psalmist brilliantly establishes the opposite to be the case. Language normally employed to worship Baal for the awesome might of the thunderstorm did not rightfully belong to him who was no true god. Such language belonged to the God of Israel alone. And so in Psalm 29, imitating so closely the language of the Canaanites, we receive an insight vital to the religion of the Hebrews. God is not limited to the sphere of history; he must be worshipped also as Lord of nature. It would be mistaken to think that Baal had any real power over nature, as generations of Canaanites had believed; Baal was nothing. But "the Lord sits enthroned as King for eternity" (verse 10).

The thrust and fundamental meaning of Psalm 29 were clear enough before the discovery of the Ugaritic texts, and yet something new has been provided. The reader of the psalm now knows a little more of the background, of the subtle forces that tended to detract from the true worship of the Lord. Psalm 29 is not merely a psalm praising God as the Lord of nature. It is a psalm which rings out that praise in a world dominated by the belief that nature was the domain of Baal.

2. Amos the "Shepherd"

One of the continuing puzzles in biblical scholarship has been the attempt to determine something about the nature of Amos' profession before he began his short prophetic ministry. Amos came from the region of Tekoa, a few miles south of Bethlehem; it was there that he lived and worked during the latter half of the eighth century B.C. In the account of his vocation, it is said that he was a cattleman and fruit farmer (Amos 7:14-15); the fruit was probably the rather sour, figlike fruit that grows on a type of mulberry tree on the shores of the Dead Sea. In addition to these two slender pieces of information, we are also told that Amos was a *nōqēd*, a word which is usually translated as "shepherd." But in the Old Testament as a whole the normal term for shepherd is not *nōqēd*, but rather *rōʻeh*. In fact, apart from its use in Amos 1:1, the Hebrew word is used in only one other passage in the entire Old Testament; it is employed in 2 Kings 3:4 to describe King Mesha of Moab. It is the rarity of the word's use in the Old Testament which has created some general uncertainty as to its precise meaning.

Among the first Ugaritic texts to be discovered were the various large tablets containing the Baal cycle. One of the Baal texts contains at the end a colophon, indicating that it was written by the scribe called Ilmilku, who is described as a "disciple of *Atn.prln*, chief of priests, chief of shepherds"; the Ugaritic word translated "shepherd" is *nqd*, linguistically the precise equivalent of Hebrew *nōqēd*. The Ugaritic text, taken alone, might suggest that the "shepherds," along with the "priests," were groups of religious personnel, for the text strongly indicates that they were the servants of the temple and its high priest.

This possibility has been exploited by a number of Scandinavian scholars. On the basis of the Ugaritic evidence, they have suggested that "shepherdship" had some kind of sacral character. The specific type of shepherd called *nqd* not only looked after the temple flocks, but was probably also involved in the preparation of sheep for sacrifice. Thus, on the basis of the Ugaritic evidence, these scholars proposed that Amos too may have been a temple servant, looking after the flocks of the Jerusalem temple and being involved in its sacrifices.

If this hypothesis could be sustained, it would be particularly important for the interpretation of Amos' message. Amos was a citizen of the southern state of Judah, but his short ministry took place in the northern state of Israel. And in Israel, Amos made the famous statement that he was neither a prophet nor a prophet's son (Amos 7:14), which is usually taken to mean that he was not a cultic prophet, or a servant of the temple. But if Amos were indeed a servant of the Jerusalem temple, as the Scandinavian scholars have suggested, then his critique of religion and society in the northern state of Israel must be interpreted in the light of his official connections.

It is almost certain, however, that the Scandinavian scholars were wrong in their hypothesis; their error lay principally in examining only one of the Ugaritic texts in which the word *nqd* is used. The text they used did indeed indicate that the word *nqd* had religious associations. But the word is also used in nine other Ugaritic texts, and two further Akkadian texts from Ugarit; that set of evidence, taken as a whole, strongly indicates that the use of *nqd* in the colophon of the Baal text is atypical. The other texts in which the word *nqd* is used indicate that these Ugaritic "shepherds" formed a distinctive social group. Their most important characteristic was that they were royal dependents, servants of the royal palace (and the group working for the temple were a minority, unusual in having responsibility to the high priest). These "shepherds" were liable to direct military service on behalf of the king, but could also receive particular privileges from the king, such as land grants. Like other persons, they had to pay taxes, but the fiscal law is clear in indicating that they held a relatively high status in Ugaritic society. In summary, the Ugaritic evidence indicates that the *nqdm* were men of some position and influence. They were not simple, working shepherds, but managers of large herds; they were probably also engaged in the marketing of sheep products.

It is this general background which should more appropriately be used to interpret the background to Amos' professional life. When we read that Amos was a shepherd, it is easy to conjure up in the mind a simple pastoral image, and then to marvel at his powers of speech and mind as we read the words he spoke. But it is probably more accurate to think of Amos the *nōqēd* as being similar to the Ugaritic *nqd*; he probably owned, or managed, large herds of sheep and was engaged in the marketing of their products. Indeed, it was probably his marketing duties that took him north from his home state of Judah to the market towns of Israel, there to sell his goods. Taken together, the evidence indicates that Amos was engaged extensively in agricultural business, being involved in cattle and fruit-farming, in addition to sheep.

And it was from this large and responsible position that Amos was called to be a prophet, a vocation to which he responded willingly.

3. On Cooking a Kid in Milk (Deuteronomy 14:21)

The laws of Moses contain numerous passages which are obscure and strange to the modern reader. The main themes of the law are well known; they relate to morality, to sacrifice and ceremony, and to various religious and secular matters. But there are many other passages which seem out of place; the law provides instructions concerning what to do when a bird's nest is found in the countryside (Deuteronomy 22:6-7), concerning the location of tassels on a cloak (verse 12), and other matters of uncertain significance in our modern world.

One of the strangest portions of the law is found in Deuteronomy 14:21 (and Exodus 23:19): "You shall not boil a kid in its mother's milk." Why, one is tempted to ask, would an Israelite ever have even contemplated boiling a kid in its mother's milk? It is unlikely that we will ever understand the prohibition unless we first understand the meaning of the act. Many centuries ago, Maimonides, a great Jewish exegete and philosopher, had a suggestion as to the meaning of the prohibition, which he recorded in his work, *The Guide for the Perplexed* (*circa* 1195):

> "meat boiled in milk is undoubtedly gross food, and makes overfull; but I think that most probably it is also prohibited because it is somehow connected with idolatry, forming perhaps part of the service, or being used on some festival of the heathen. . . ."

Maimonides' explanation rings true, but he himself admitted that he could find no evidence to support it from the ancient books of religious rites which were known to him. Hence, the discovery of Ras Shamra in the twentieth century offered new promise; perhaps this fresh source of insight concerning the religion of the Canaanites would provide a clue to the meaning of an ancient piece of Mosaic law.

In 1933, Charles Virolleaud published in French an edition of one of the newly discovered Ugaritic clay tablets; he entitled the text "The birth of the gracious and beautiful gods." The text was religious in nature. One side contained a number of religious and ritual directions; the other contained a story of the god El and elaborated on some of his sexual escapades. The story contained on the tablet was thought to lie behind the religious activity described in its opening lines.

Although the tablet was fairly well preserved, some portions of it were hard to read because of surface damage. Line 14, on the first side, was difficult to read, but Virolleaud conjectured its sense and translated the line as follows: "cook a kid in milk." He admitted the conjectural nature of his reading and drew no conclusions from it. Two years later, Harold L. Ginsberg published a study of the same Ugaritic text. He followed Virolleaud in the reading of line 14, and then he drew attention to the fact that this text provided illumination of the biblical law (Deuteronomy 14:21) and appeared to substantiate Maimonides' suggestion concerning its meaning.

Since 1935 a large number of scholars have followed the interpretation of Ginsberg and perceived in this text illumination of the background of Hebrew law. It is a tempting view to take, for its implications would be as follows. The Canaanite (Ugaritic) text appears to describe some kind of ritual which related to fertility and sexuality; it is possible that the ritual involved sexual activity by the participants. The cooking of a kid in milk would simply be one small part of the larger ritual. With this background, the obscure law in Deuteronomy 14:21 would take on considerable significance. The Hebrew law simply prohibits the cooking of a kid in its mother's milk. To the modern reader, that is obscure; to the ancient Israelite, however, the association would be clear. The simple prohibition bars something larger; it prohibits that kind of religious ceremony, practiced among the Canaanites, which maintained a view of sexuality, human and divine, which was anathema to the Hebrews. What the law really prohibits, then, is religious practices akin to those of the Canaanites, practices which might appeal to human nature but which were outlawed by divine law.

Perhaps it was because this Ugaritic background to biblical law made such good sense that it lasted for so long after its initial proposal by Ginsberg in 1935. In fact, however, this is an example of the kind of blind alleys into which the Ugaritic texts have sometimes led biblical scholars. There are a number of reasons why this particular Ugaritic text must be rejected as illuminating the world of Hebrew law. First, and most obviously, the biblical law prohibits cooking a kid in its *mother's* milk; the Ugaritic text makes no reference to "mother." Second, even if Virolleaud's conjecture concerning the reading of the text is accepted, the translation he offered cannot be accepted; the word translated "cook" almost certainly means "slaughter." But most importantly, it now appears that Virolleaud's conjecture as to the reading of the line was wrong, and that the text in question must be translated in a totally different fashion.

Now these comments are not intended to be critical of Virolleaud, Ginsberg, and other scholars. It is necessary in pioneering studies to engage in conjecture and intelligent guesswork. But as the insights of earlier scholars are tested and examined, some are rejected and others are retained. This particular suggestion has been rejected; we do not have any clear Ugaritic illumination of Deuteronomy 14:21.

And yet we conclude this section with a gentle irony. Maimonides' suggestion is as likely today as it was when he first proposed it. And although the Ugaritic texts have not provided precise illumination of the ancient biblical law, it remains highly likely that the biblical text prohibits something central to the religion of Canaan and Ugarit.

4. Psalm 104: A Cosmopolitan Hymn

For a long time, Psalm 104 has fascinated scholars engaged in the comparative study of biblical literature. It is a classical psalm, expressing in lyrical poetry the same wonders of creation that are recounted more prosaically in Genesis 1. Perhaps because of its creation theme, it has invited comparison with other ancient texts devoted to the same topic.

The comparisons drawn by earlier scholars were of a general nature and were not intended to be the basis of any particular hypothesis. In 1753, Bishop Robert Lowth, who was professor of poetry at Oxford University, published his famous *Lectures on the Sacred Poetry of the Hebrews*. In those lectures, he drew a number of comparisons between biblical poetry and classical (Greek and Latin) poetry. With respect to Psalm 104, he could think of only one approximate comparison; a hymn of the Stoic Cleanthes almost measured up to the excellence and sublimity of the Hebrew psalm.

In the years that followed, other scholars, such as Herder in Germany, drew general parallels between Psalm 104 and non-biblical literature. But during the first decade of the twentieth century, a change came about in the comparative study of the psalm. That change was prompted by the excavation of the archives of Tell el-Amarna in Egypt in the late nineteenth and early twentieth centuries; that discovery, and later the discovery of rock tombs from the Amarna Age, opened for investigation the literature of that remarkable pharaoh, Akhenaten. One of the Egyptian texts which was rediscovered was a sun-hymn attributed to Akhenaten.

Writing in 1905, J. H. Breasted, one of the most famous American Egyptologists, called attention to the close similarities between Psalm 104 and the sun-hymn of Akhenaten. Some years later, encouraged by the similar observations of the German scholar, Hugo Gressmann, Breasted took an even firmer stand; the Egyptian hymn revealed the source of the Hebrew psalmist's recognition of the goodness of God in creation. Almost all scholars since that time have recognized the similarities between the psalm and Akhenaten's hymn, though few of them would nowadays accept the possibility of a direct link between the two passages. Psalm 104 was similar not only to Akhenaten's sun-hymn, but also to many other Egyptian hymns addressed to the sun. And if the basis of comparisons is broadened, numerous parallels can be seen between the psalm and such texts as the Babylonian hymns dedicated to the sun-god, Shamash. The increase in the number of parallels between Psalm 104 and other Near Eastern texts reduced the probability that the Hebrew psalm was dependent on some earlier texts, but highlighted nevertheless the cosmopolitan nature of the psalm.

The Ugaritic texts provide further light on the character of Psalm 104, especially in its opening verses. The language of the biblical poet, in these verses, bears a number of striking resemblances to the language employed in one of the stories concerning Baal. The Hebrew psalmist describes the Lord as "the One who makes the clouds his chariot" (verse 3); Baal is described as the "rider of the clouds." In the psalm, "fire and flame" are personifications of the ministers of the Lord (verse 4); in the Baal text, "fire and flame" are employed in the preparation of silver and gold for the building of Baal's palace. The voice of the Lord (verse 7) and the voice of Baal are both likened to thunder. Psalm 104:16 refers to the cedars of Lebanon, and in the Ugaritic text wood from Lebanon was employed in the construction of Baal's palace. The Hebrew psalmist describes the Lord as watering the mountains from his heavenly abode; the Ugaritic poet describes an opening in Baal's palace through which he would water the earth.

These, and other similarities, exist between Psalm 104 and the Ugaritic literature. But how are they to be explained? And what explanation is possible that will also take into account the parallels between the psalm and Egyptian hymns, not to mention Babylonian hymns? The interpretation of such evidence is always somewhat speculative, but an hypothesis is possible.

It is very likely that Psalm 104 is a product of the age of Solomon, one of the most cosmopolitan periods in the history of the Hebrews. The beginning of Solomon's reign was characterized not only by strength in a political and national sense, but it was also a time when Jerusalem was a center of cultural interchange (1 Kings 4:34; 10:1). It was a time for the exchange of ideas, for broad vision and international spirit. But this was also the period in which the first temple was built, and it is significant to note that the Hebrews employed Phoenician (Canaanite) craftsmen in the construction of their temple.

It is possible, though by no means certain, that Psalm 104 was composed initially as a dedication hymn for the newly constructed temple of the Lord. Just as the new temple in Jerusalem was physically similar to other Near Eastern temples, so too Psalm 104 has similarities to other Near Eastern hymns. But the psalm makes some important and radical theological affirmations, which in turn are significant for understanding the meaning of the temple in Jerusalem. In a sense, the temple was the house of God; in a sense, it symbolized the divine presence in the midst of the people. But in Hebrew theology, God could not be limited in time and place, and it would be wrong to think of the temple as functioning literally as the home of God. The language of the psalm points to the transcendent and boundless nature of the God of Israel. All of nature owes its existence and continuity to the creative power of God.

O Lord, how manifold are your works!
In wisdom you have made them all:
The earth is full of your creations.

(Psalm 104:24)

There is thus a sense in which Psalm 104 is distinctively Hebrew; there is another sense in which it is "everyman's psalm."
In language of remarkable beauty and profundity, it extols the
creative power of the God whose house had been built in Jerusalem, but it does so in such a fashion that others could hear and
understand. Its words would create a sense of recognition in the
ears of Egyptians and Canaanites, but its message focused firmly
on the one true God. The temple, not in itself unique, and the
psalm, thoroughly cosmopolitan, together point beyond themselves to the totally unique, the God of Israel.

5. The Musical Background to the Psalms

The book of Psalms is the hymnbook of the Old Testament. It
contains diverse types of material, including prayers and liturgies;
but many of its passages are hymns that would have been sung
originally within the setting of Israel's worship. While the words
of the psalms are known, the musical settings and arrangements
to which they were sung remain unknown. A certain amount is
known in theory about Israelite music, for the biblical text makes
numerous references to musical instruments and orchestras. But
no amount of theory is an adequate substitute for hearing the actual
sound of music, and the sounds of Israel's hymns seemed until
recently to be lost in perpetuity.

There is a limit to how far one can go back in tracing the
manner in which the psalms were sung. There are some notations
in the Massoretic text of the Hebrew Bible which provide clues
as to their musical performance, but these clues pertain to the
singing of the psalms in the era of the Massoretic scribes, namely
the first few centuries A.D. They give no firm evidence with
respect to the biblical period as such. Some slightly firmer evidence can be gained from the titles that are prefixed to many
biblical psalms, for many of these appear to contain musical notations. The expression *sheminith* in the title of Psalm 6 may refer
to the octave, and the phrase "the Hind of Dawn" in the title of

Psalm 22 may be the name of a musical tune. There are many other such items of information in the psalm titles which almost certainly have something to do with music, but still the fact remains that we have no idea of the sound of the music that would have accompanied the singing of the psalms. Indeed, the oldest extant evidence of the sound of music comes not from the ancient Near Eastern civilizations, but from the Classical World of the early centuries B.C.

Once again, it is the evidence that has been excavated from ancient Ugarit that has radically changed the picture and provided new insight into the early history of music. During the months of November and December 1951, the excavations of the fifteenth campaign were focused on the royal palace of Ugarit; among the various texts that were found that season were two fragmentary texts numbered 15.30 and 15.49, respectively. Two seasons later, during the excavations conducted between September and December 1953, a further fragment of a tablet in very poor condition was found, also in the palace area, and was numbered 17.387. Some years later, the French scholar Emmanuel Laroche recognized that these three fragments were part of a single text, and that they fitted together perfectly like the parts of a jigsaw puzzle. The reconstructed tablet was rectangular in shape, some three inches deep and about 7.5 inches wide. Laroche published his version of the text in the official publication of the French archaeological mission, *Ugaritica* 5 (1968).

When the tablet was reconstructed, it was then in a form suitable for examination by a variety of scholars. The tablet was unusual, beginning with four lines of writing which extended round to the back of the tablet. But on the face of the tablet, two horizontal lines had been drawn in the clay underneath the first four lines of writing, and beneath the two horizontal lines were seven further lines of symbols. An examination of the text revealed that the first four lines of writing contained the words of an ancient hymn or cult song. The lines beneath the central division of the text indicated the musical accompaniment to which the song was to be sung. The song itself was written in the Hurrian language (the Hurrians are referred to frequently in the Old Testament as the Horites: e.g., Deuteronomy 2:12). The musical accompaniment was to be played on a lyre. Thus this ancient, reconstructed clay tablet from Ugarit contained the oldest surviving evidence of the nature of music in the world, moving back the date of the evidence for ancient music by more than a millennium. But still the music could not be heard.

The next stage in the story was unravelled by three American scholars: Anne Draffkorn Kilmer, an Assyriologist; Richard L. Crocker, a musicologist; and Robert R. Brown, a physicist. First, a theoretical understanding had to be developed of the nature of ancient musical symbols and terms, which would make possible the interpretation of the musical portion of the Hurrian hymn text. This was done by the examination of some ancient Babylonian musical texts, which provided not only a theoretical account of musical forms in old Babylon, but also described how a lyre was to be tuned. Then two lyres were built, patterned on ancient lyres, employing archaeological and inscriptional data as a guide to the construction. The first model was based on the remains of a Sumerian lyre which had been excavated by Sir Leonard Woolley at Ur in 1927. The second was patterned on a Palestinian lyre depicted on an ivory inlay that had been excavated at Megiddo, a place that is closer both culturally and geographically to Ugarit. These modern replicas were then tuned according to the principles contained in the Old Babylonian tuning texts. Thus equipped, the American scholars were able to sing, with lyre accompaniment, the ancient Hurrian cult song that at one time had been used in religious worship in Ugarit. Kilmer, Crocker, and Brown recorded their reconstruction of this ancient music on a stereo record, entitled *Sounds from Silence*; to hear it is to hear haunting sounds from the past.

There is a sense in which the extraordinary rediscovery of ancient Ugarit's music helps to bridge the gap between our modern world and the musical world of the Psalms. Of course, there can be no certainty that this modern recording of ancient music is precise and accurate, and even if there were, we do not know the extent to which Hebrew music was similar to Hurrian music. But almost certainly there would have been some degree of similarity. The Hurrians were scattered throughout the Near East, and certainly they were not unknown to the Hebrews. And indeed, in religious matters, there is some evidence to suggest that there were similarities between the religion of the Hurrians and that of Israel (see section 6, below). Thus, in listening to a modern record of an ancient Hurrian hymn, we are able to enter in a partial fashion into the musical world of the Hebrews, and to sense tentatively something of the sound of the Hebrews' praise of their God.

6. Hurrians, Hebrews, and the God of Covenant

Central to the theology of the Old Testament is the identification of God with the idea of covenant. In a formal sense, Israel's religion was established in the covenant made between the people and God at Mt. Sinai in the time of Moses. Prior to the event at Sinai, the Hebrews were slaves in Egypt, where they were bound to their Egyptian masters by a covenant or contract (for which the Egyptian word was *bryt*). The Exodus from Egypt marked the liberation of the Hebrew people from their covenant of slavery to the pharaoh; the occasion of Sinai was marked by the taking on of a new covenant (called *berît* in Hebrew), one of complete obedience to the Lord. And the centrality of this theme throughout the rest of the Bible is indicated by its title; the rather antique expression "Old Testament" may be translated literally "Old Covenant."

Perhaps because of the centrality of the biblical concept of God and covenant, a number of scholars have claimed this to be one of the unique and distinctive characteristics of Israel's religion. Certainly it appeared to be true that no other religion in the ancient Near East linked a god or gods so closely to the notion of covenant as was the case in Israel. Yet there is always a certain risk in claiming uniqueness, for very often some evidence turns up to undermine the claim. In this case, the evidence was discovered in Ugarit.

During the twenty-fourth campaign, conducted in the fall of 1961, a number of texts were found in the area south of the acropolis. One of these was of particular interest; it was written in the Hurrian language and contained an invocational hymn to various gods worshipped by the Hurrians. In the fourteenth and fifteenth lines of this text, there appeared an expression that was odd in the Hurrian language: "*el brt . el dn*." The words appeared to be Semitic loan words (viz., Ugaritic words) employed in the Hurrian text, and the occurrence of loan words was not in principle surprising, for the Hurrians in Ugarit would certainly have been bilingual, speaking both Hurrian and Ugaritic. The latter part of the expression is clear: *el dn* must mean "El (or god) of judgment." The first part of the expression, however, was translated by Emmanuel Laroche as "El of springs." That translation was possible, though the word for "springs, wells" in Ugaritic is spelled *b'r(t)*, not *brt*, which led to some suspicion as to the correctness of Laroche's rendering. On further examination, it became reasonably certain that the expression in the Hurrian hymn must be translated: "El of covenant, El of judgment."

When this expression from an ancient Hurrian hymn is set in a wider context, it takes on particular significance. Outside of the Near East, there is one religion which does possess a central identification of a god with covenant; it is the ancient religion of India, as it is reflected in the scripture of that religion, the Rig Veda. In an ancient Vedic hymn, Mithra is praised as the deification of covenant; and in numerous hymns, both Mithra and Varuna are praised as gods of judgment. The Vedic religion of India may seem to be a great distance away from the religion of Ugarit and Israel, but the distance is not all that great. There is considerable overlap between the religion of the Hittites and Hurrians, on the one hand, and the Vedic religion on the other hand. Both religious traditions seem to stem from a mass movement of peoples in the third millennium B.C. from west to east; some settled in Anatolia, and others moved on to South Asia. And the commonality of tradition can be seen in the names of gods. Mithra was worshipped in Anatolia as well as India; Varuna of India is known in Hittite texts as Urwana. In all probability the Hurrians worshipped both these gods.

The reference in the Hurrian hymn to "El of covenant, El of judgment" is probably a reflection of the process of syncretism taking place. The high god Mithra and the high god El became fused into one in the Hurrian religion, creating an expression which happens to parallel the religion of Israel. And no doubt this syncretism spread far beyond the boundaries of the kingdom of Ugarit. In Palestine, far to the south, there is a pre-Hebrew place name, El-berith, in the vicinity of Shechem (Judges 9:46), which probably reflects the spread of the concept of "El of covenant" in the Canaanite world.

In this example, the religious conceptions held in Ugarit have simply illustrated further the milieu in which the biblical religion developed. The Hebrews were not unique in associating their God with covenant. The content of their conception, however, was entirely unique. The covenant God of Israel was not the essence of an abstract belief; it was the historical events of Exodus and Sinai which provided the entire substance of the notion of covenant. The God who had delivered Israel from slavery, by breaking the Egyptian *bryt*, had entered into a personal *berît* with his chosen people.

7. "Ships" in Judges 5:17?

In the original written form of the Hebrew text of the Bible words were spelled only with consonants, for the oldest Hebrew alphabet did not have symbols to represent the vowels. The absence of vowels would have caused few, if any, difficulties for the original users of the script, for their knowledge of the living language would have enabled them to know both the pronunciation and meaning of the written words. But one of the consequences of this mode of writing is the presence of a number of homographs in Hebrew texts; a homograph is a single written form which represents two different words (or more) which may have been pronounced differently but would have been written identically in the consonantal script. The meanings of a homograph can usually be distinguished on the basis of context, provided that both meanings are known in the first place. There are a number of terms in old Hebrew, however, that are not clearly recognized as homographs. One meaning may be common and well known, while the second may have been lost with the passage of time.

An example of this phenomenon may be seen in Judges 5:17. The verse is a part of one of the oldest surviving texts in the Hebrew language, the Song of Deborah (Judges 5:1-31), which contains many obscurities as a consequence of its antiquity. Verse 17 is commonly translated as follows (RSV):

> Gilead stayed beyond the Jordan;
>   and Dan, why did he abide with the ships?
> Asher sat still on the coast of the sea,
>   settling down by his landings.

The larger context is that of a series of condemnations addressed to the various tribes that did not send volunteers to assist Deborah in her battle against the Canaanites. But the second line of the verse is puzzling. At face value it makes good sense, but what does it really mean to say that the tribe of Dan remained "with the ships"? So far as is known, the Danites never resided in a region by the sea, nor did they ever engage in maritime activity, as the line indicates. The puzzle lies in the fact that the typical activity of the Danites as described in this line does not fit any of their known activities. The problem lies in the word "ships," spelled in Hebrew consonantal writing as *'nywt*.

A possible resolution to the problem may lie in the observation that *'nywt* is probably a homograph; but if such is the case, the second meaning of the word is not known elsewhere in the Hebrew Bible. Again, some evidence suggesting a solution has been found in the Ugaritic texts. In three Ugaritic texts there occurs the word *'an* (and also the form *'any*). The fact that the word occurs in three different texts makes it reasonably easy to ascertain its meaning. The Ugaritic word *'an* means "to relax, be at ease." But what is particularly interesting about the Ugarit evidence is that in one of the texts, the word *'an* is used in association with the Ugaritic verb *gr* "to remain." The fact is interesting because this is the Ugaritic form of the Hebrew verb (*gwr*) which is used in Judges 5:17. The Hebrew text has the verb *gwr* followed by the mysterious *'nywt*; the Ugaritic text has *gr* followed by *'an* (both Hebrew and Ugaritic terms being linguistically equivalent).

In the light of the Ugaritic evidence, a new translation of the Hebrew verse becomes possible.

> Gilead stayed beyond the Jordan;
> and Dan, why did he abide at ease?
> Asher sat still on the coast of the sea,
> settling down by his landings.

If this rendition of the verse is correct, as seems highly probable, it is an interesting example of the way in which new knowledge enables a better translation of the ancient text. The early translators faced the problem of how to render *'nywt*; the word looked like "ships" and the use of the word "sea" in the next line seemed to add weight to the translation. But, in fact, *'nywt* is an extremely ancient word, a homograph at the time it was written. And as the centuries passed and the language changed, the second sense of the word dropped out of common usage and gradually was forgotten. It was only the rediscovery of the Ugaritic language that made it

possible to rediscover this lost meaning and to translate Judges
5:17 in an appropriate fashion. It is a very minor correction and
does little to change the general sense of the Old Testament; it is
only when one multiplies this example a few hundred times that
one begins to perceive the far-reaching effects that a knowledge
of Ugaritic has for the translation of Hebrew.

8. Ugarit, Israel, and the Greeks

The Ugaritic texts are important not only for the study of biblical
texts, but also for the study of the background to early Greek
thought and mythology. It is recognized increasingly that the principal genius of early Greek civilization lay not so much in cre-
ativity, as in the genius of adaptation. And not least may this
genius be seen in the manner in which early Greek mythology
reflects to a large extent the adaptation of the earlier themes and
stories of Near Eastern mythology. Among the principal avenues
through which this knowledge of Near Eastern mythology passed
over to the Mycenaean and early Greek world was Ugarit; that
ancient city was located in the Near East, but its coastal situation
and its involvement in maritime trade made it also an outlet for
Near Eastern culture into the Mediterranean world.

One of the consequences of this new understanding of the background to Greek civilization is that it necessitates a reappraisal of
some older hypotheses concerning Greek influence in the Old
Testament literature. A case in point may be found in Isaiah
14:12-14. The Hebrew poet addresses a taunt song to the king
of Babylon, whose military might and arrogance had led him to
commit the crime of hubris: "I will make myself like the Most
High!" (verse 14). In the taunting parody of the Babylonian king,
the author calls him "*Helel*, Son of Dawn." The Hebrew word
hêlēl means "shining one"; this and other features of the poetry
led a number of scholars to suggest that the mythological background of the poetry was to be found in the Greek myth of
Phaethon. Phaethon, in the Greek story, was the "shining" son
of Helios, who attempted to drive his father's golden chariot but
was unable to control the massive power of its horses. The parallel
is constructive, for like Phaethon the Babylonian king attempted
to assert powers that were too great for him; his inadequacy would
result in his doom.

There were grave difficulties with the proposed Greek antecedents of the Hebrew text, however, not least of which was the problem of chronology. While it is not easy to date Isaiah 14 with precision, it is generally assumed to be older than the surviving forms of the Greek Phaethon story. In chronological terms, it is more probable that the Old Testament influenced early Greek literature than vice versa. Hence, it is not surprising that a number of scholars turned to the Ugaritic texts in the search for the literary antecedents to Isaiah 14. It seemed probable that the author of that passage had employed an ancient and familiar story to parody the aspirations and might of the Babylonian king.

The Ugaritic background to the story is to be found in the texts concerning Baal; a part of the great Baal narrative concerns the god Athtar, who in a brief interregnum attempts to fill Baal's throne. Athtar, in the Ugaritic texts, is called the "Luminous One," and reference is made to his "shining," which is a direct parallel to the name *Helel*, "Shining One," employed in Isaiah. But it is also significant that in the Ugaritic texts, Athtar is identified as a warrior god, making still more precise the parallel between him and the arrogant Babylonian king. The essence of the parallel, however, is to be found in the inadequacy of Athtar. He attempts to fill the throne of the great god Baal during his absence, but he is too small for the throne and his feet do not reach the ground, symbolizing his inability to exercise the powers of Baal. The essence of the background is essentially inadequacy; just as Athtar could not fill Baal's throne, so too the Babylonian king could not exercise the divine powers that he claimed for himself. And if it can be assumed that the amusing story of Athtar was well known to Isaiah's audience, then the power of the parody of this Babylonian potentate is all the more evident.

This particular exercise in comparison is informative in a number of ways. It illustrates the manner in which a Hebrew poet could draw on the cultural resources of his world to make an effective point with his audience. Only when we know what they knew (in this case, the story of Athtar), are we in a position to appreciate the power of the language that is used in the biblical text. But more than that, it becomes clear that parts of biblical literature and Greek mythology share a common heritage, that of Near Eastern civilization and literature, as it is reflected in the texts from Ugarit. The story of Athtar is not only the source of Isaiah's parody, but also the origin of the Greek story of Phaethon.

9. Baal and the Exodus

The Exodus was one of the foundational events of Israel's religion. It marked the liberation from Egyptian slavery, which in turn made possible the formation of a relationship of covenant between Israel and God. And nowhere is the Exodus given more powerful expression than in the Song of the Sea (Exodus 15:1-18), a great victory hymn celebrating God's triumph over Egypt at the sea. To this day, the ancient hymn continues to be employed in the synagogue worship of Judaism. Its continued use reflects the centrality of its theme, that of God's control over the forces of both nature and history in the redemption of his people.

When one reads the Song of the Sea, one immediately gains an impression of the joy and exhilaration expressed by those who first used its words in worship. But what is not immediately evident to the modern reader is the subtle manner in which the poet has given force to his themes by the adaptation of Canaanite mythology. Underlying the words and structure of the Hebrew hymn are the motifs of the central mythology of Baal; only when one understands the fashion in which that mythology has been transformed can one go on to perceive the extraordinary significance which the poet attributed to the Exodus from Egypt.

The poet has applied some of the most central motifs of the myth of Baal. These motifs may be summarized in certain key terms: conflict, order, kingship, and palace-construction. Taking the cycle of Baal texts as a whole (see further Chapter IV), the narrative begins with conflict between Baal and Yamm ("Sea"); Baal, representing order, is threatened by the chaotic Yamm. Baal's conquest of Yamm marks one of the steps in the process of creation; order is established, and chaos is subdued. Baal's victory over Yamm is also the key to his kingship, and to symbolize the order and consolidate the kingship, Baal initiates the construction of his palace. And then, in the course of the myth, conflict breaks out again, this time between Baal and Mot. Baal is eventually victorious in this conflict, establishing once again his kingship and the rule of order. It is important to note not only the centrality of these motifs in the Baal myth, but also their significance; the motifs as a whole establish a cosmological framework within which to interpret the Baal myth. It is, above all, a cosmology, developing the origins and permanent establishment of order in the world, as understood and believed by the Canaanites. Its central celebration is that of creation.

In the Song of the Sea, the poet has developed the same central motifs in the structure of his song. The song begins with conflict between God and Egypt (Exodus 15:1-12), but the way in which the poet has transformed the ancient motifs is instructive. "Sea" is no longer the adversary of order, but God uses the sea (Hebrew *yam*) as an instrument in the conquest of chaos. After the conquest, God is victorious and establishes order; his kingship is proclaimed in a statement of his incomparability (verse 11). But then the theme of conflict is resumed again, as future enemies are anticipated (verses 14-16). They, too, would be conquered, and eventually God's palace and throne would be established as a symbol of the order achieved in his victory (verse 17). Finally, God's kingship would be openly declared, as a consequence of his victories: "the Lord shall reign for ever and ever" (verse 18). The Hebrew expression for this statement of kingship is *yhwh ymlk*, directly analogous to the celebration of Baal's kingship in the Ugaritic texts: *b'l ymlk*.

It is one thing to trace the motifs of the Baal myth in the Song of the Sea; it is another to grasp their significance. The primary significance lies in the cosmological meaning of the motifs; the Hebrew poet has taken the symbolic language of creation and adapted it to give expression to his understanding of the meaning of the Exodus. At one level, the Exodus was simply the escape of Hebrews from Egyptian slavery; at another level, it marked a new act of divine creation. Just as Genesis 1 celebrates the creation of the world, so too Exodus 15 celebrates the creation of a new people, Israel. And when one perceives this underlying significance of the poetic language employed in the Song of the Sea, one is then in a position to understand better another portion of the biblical text, namely the reasons given for the observation of the sabbath day. There are two versions of the Ten Commandments in the Old Testament, and both give different reasons for the observation of the sabbath. In Exodus 20:11, the Hebrews are enjoined to observe the sabbath on the basis of God's creation of the world. But in the second version, Deuteronomy 5:15, the sabbath is to be observed in commemoration of the Exodus from Egypt. At first sight the two reasons given for the observation of the same commandment seem very different, but the new understanding of the Song of the Sea, in its Canaanite/Ugaritic background, indicates just how close the two reasons are. The sabbath was to be observed, first in celebration of the creation of the world, and second in commemoration of God's creation of Israel in the Exodus. This is another of the many new insights afforded by the Ugaritic texts to the study of the Old Testament, and illustrates the manner in which an awareness of the biblical world can create a greater sensitivity in the modern reader to the power of the biblical message.

Chapter VI:
NEW DISCOVERIES
AND FUTURE
PERSPECTIVES:
Ebla and Ras Ibn Hani

DURING the period of more than fifty years since the first excavation at Ras Shamra in 1929, an enormous amount of archaeological work has been done at the site. And yet less than half of the area that was covered by the ancient city of Ugarit has been excavated. It is probable that the most significant areas of the city have been found, and also that the principal archives have already been located; nevertheless, a good deal still remains under the soil to be uncovered in future excavations at Ras Shamra under the direction of Marguerite Yon.

But if it is true that more is awaiting discovery under the soil at Ras Shamra, it is equally true that in the general area of Latakia and the coastal plain of Syria there are numerous tells, or hills, that have not been explored at all. The virgin surfaces of these tells may keep their treasures for future generations. Gabriel Saadé, an Ugaritic specialist who lives in Latakia, has estimated that there are more than thirty such tells, most of which have never been exposed to archaeological exploration other than a cursory surface survey. Many of these tells, no doubt, hide the remains of the small towns and villages which constituted the real strength of the small kingdom of Ugarit. Such towns and villages are known in some detail from the economic and administrative texts discovered at Ugarit, but their precise location and nature remain unknown.

From time to time, excavations at other sites in Syria have revealed links with the civilization and culture of Ugarit. Some British archaeologists, under the leadership of M. J. Parr, undertook an exploratory excavation in September 1975 at Tell Nebī

Mend (the ancient Kadesh on the Orontes). During the course of the excavation, they found a piece of broken pottery containing ten and a half cuneiform signs; the writing was from the same general period as the writing from Ras Shamra. With a few minor exceptions, the cuneiform signs were those familiar from the Ugaritic alphabet; they read, however, from right-to-left, rather than the left-to-right sequence that is standard in the Ugaritic texts. Minor, but significant, discoveries of this nature have been found at various other locations in Syria and Palestine, including Sarepta, Tell Sukas, Kamid el-Loz, Beth-shemesh, and Tell Ta'annak. The Ugaritic script, or a form of it, was in use not only in the general region of Syria but as far south as the territory which is part of the modern state of Israel.

Apart from discoveries of texts in Ugaritic-type writing from sites other than Ras Shamra, there have been a few discoveries indicating links between Ugarit and the rest of the Middle Eastern world. One of the most interesting such discoveries in recent years was made in Israel in the mid-1970s. A series of excavations were undertaken in the vicinity of Tell Aphek, jointly sponsored by Bar Ilan University and Tel Aviv University. The excavators came across the remains of an ancient Egyptian fortress, which had been destroyed by the Sea Peoples around 1200 B.C. In the debris of this ancient fortress, they found a clay tablet (about 9 × 5 centimeters) bearing Akkadian writing. The tablet contained a letter from a person called Takukhlina, who lived in Ugarit, to Haya, who was at that time the Egyptian ruler of a portion of the land of Canaan. The text has forty-one lines, written on both sides of the tablet. In the letter, Takukhlina asks the Egyptian governor to investigate a problem that he had, relating to the theft of 250 measures of wheat. The Ugaritic writer refers in his letter to an accompanying gift of one hundred shekels of blue wool and ten shekels of red wool, intended no doubt to encourage the investigations of Haya! Discoveries of this kind help to set a broader perspective on Ugarit's situation in the world of international affairs during the thirteenth century.

But in relative terms, the discoveries at Tell Nebī Mend and Tell Aphek are minor; they are dwarfed by two other highly significant discoveries of the last decade, both of which promise to shed further light on Ugarit's history and civilization. The first of these was the discovery of the state archives of Ebla at Tell

Mardikh in Syria. The second significant find was the rediscovery of a small Ugaritic town at Ras Ibn Hani, a suburb of modern Latakia.

1. Tell Mardikh: The Rediscovery of Ebla

The story of Ebla's rediscovery begins in 1963, but it was to be more than a decade before it came to the attention of the general public. In 1963 Paulo Matthiae began the planning for a major archaeological excavation in central Syria; he was at that time twenty-three years old and a member of the Institute of Near Eastern Studies in the University of Rome. Contrary to the advice of some senior colleagues, Matthiae determined to excavate a large mound called Tell Mardikh, about thirty miles south of Aleppo, close to the main road running south through Syria from Aleppo to Damascus. There are many such mounds or artificial hills in Syria, and most of them hide beneath the surface soil the remnants of former human habitation. The mound at Tell Mardikh is large; it rises some fifty feet above the surrounding plain and has a surface area of about 140 acres; it is in a "donut" formation, a round hill with a crater in the middle. Matthiae speculated, on the basis of the size of the tell, that it must originally have been a fairly large city, and that the crater-effect was caused by the remains of ancient city walls, protruding to a higher elevation than the central area of the city as such.

The initial campaigns at Tell Mardikh were successful, though not spectacular or particularly newsworthy. By the end of the first season of excavation, Matthiae and his team had uncovered in a preliminary fashion the remains of an urban civilization that had flourished around 2300 B.C. As the campaigns continued, more and more physical evidence was found that helped to fill out something of the character of that ancient civilization.

But it was not until the end of the 1974 season that the excavators began to unearth more spectacular finds. At that time, while removing debris from the floor of an ancient building (a palace), the first of a series of clay tablets were discovered. There were approximately forty such texts discovered at that time, dating from about 2300. However, the unusual character of the texts did not emerge until the writing as such was examined in more detail.

The Italian archaeologists called in their linguistic consultant,

Giovanni Pettinato, to examine the texts. After a short examination of the texts, Pettinato claimed (in a paper presented to a congress of Assyriologists) that some of the texts were written in a language that was formerly unknown. He called it a form of "Proto-Canaanite," indicating that it was the oldest known form of the Northwest Semitic languages, which are better known to us in later forms and dialects such as Ugaritic, Biblical Hebrew, and Moabite. The evidence for this linguistic family of languages, if Pettinato were correct, had been moved back by almost a thousand years in the discovery made in 1974.

Pettinato's claims to have rediscovered an ancient language, Proto-Canaanite, the "ancestor" of Biblical Hebrew, did not go unchallenged in the scholarly community. Indeed, in the spring of 1975 a debate was emerging which was essentially critical of Pettinato's views: not least of the criticisms leveled against him was that the evidence on which the hypothesis was based was extremely limited and fragmentary. But while the scholarly debate was emerging amongst the linguists, the Italian team continued with its excavations in 1975. During that season alone, they made the most dramatic part of a series of significant discoveries; they uncovered the palace archives of the ancient city of Ebla. In total, more than fifteen thousand clay tablets were discovered during the 1975 season, many broken and fragmentary, but some very large and in nearly perfect condition (which is extraordinary, considering that the tablets are nearly forty-five hundred years old). The following year, a further sixteen hundred tablets were discovered; since then the findings have been more slender, but the current total of recovered texts is approaching twenty thousand. It is thus almost the largest find of its kind (exceeded only by Mari) and certainly the largest discovery of texts from as far back in time as the third millennium B.C.

In any excavation of this kind, the discovery of written texts is extremely important. The recovery of artifacts and the laying bare of ancient structures provide, as it were, the skeleton of an ancient civilization; it is only when written texts are discovered that the skeleton can be clothed in flesh and life breathed into the ancient remains. The texts describe what people in that ancient society were really like, what they thought and believed, how they behaved and conducted business, what they knew, and how their society functioned. The huge collection of texts from the archives of ancient Ebla provides an insight into life in that civilization; there are literary and religious texts, financial and administrative texts, royal and military texts, and even bilingual dictionaries.

As this vast collection was examined by Pettinato, he found that while many were written in Sumerian (a language already well known from other discoveries in the Near East), approximately twenty percent of texts (or more than three thousand) were written in the formerly unknown language that he had identified tentatively as "Proto-Canaanite." The texts in the formerly unknown language were written in cuneiform, so that there was no puzzle of decipherment to be solved. The language was sufficiently similar to other Semitic languages to permit Pettinato to make sense of the texts fairly quickly. But he was helped enormously by the bilingual dictionaries. One such text contained approximately one thousand words in the newly-discovered language (called Eblaite, after the city in which it was used), listed in columns; in parallel columns, the meaning of those words was given in Sumerian. Thus the archives provided not only evidence of a lost language, but also the essential tool by which the language could be translated and interpreted. (Eighteen copies of one bilingual dictionary were found, indicating that it was the ancient equivalent of a modern "best-seller.")

When the evidence was assembled (and the process still continues), it became clear that the city of Ebla had been the capital city of an empire in central Syria that had flourished in the latter part of the third millennium B.C. The population, as was common at that time, had been spread throughout the country towns and rural areas. The capital city is estimated to have had a population of approximately twenty-three thousand; half of this population, according to one of the administrative texts, were directly involved in the imperial bureaucracy! But it is our new knowledge of the existence of this large and flourishing empire that is making it necessary to rewrite much of the early history of the Near East. For prior to this discovery, it was thought that the principal center of early civilization was in Southern Iraq/Mesopotamia, and was Sumerian in character; it is now clear that there was a flourishing civilization in the north that was Semitic in character and language, as early as the third millennium.

Turning to the implications of this discovery for an understanding of Ugarit and the biblical world, it should be stressed that inevitably there remains the element of uncertainty and controversy. As Pettinato began to examine the contents of the clay tablets, he made certain claims (both written and oral) which naturally evoked considerable fresh interest in the relevance of the discovery. A few examples follow.

(a) Many of the Ebla texts contain names, Semitic in character, which are already familiar: "anglicized" examples include David, Abram, Esau, Saul, Benjamin. The names sound "biblical," as indeed they are, though (with the exception of David) they are common Semitic names. David, apart from the texts from Ebla, is known only in the biblical literature.

(b) In a list of Eblaite monarchs, one of the kings who had reigned in ancient Ebla was called Ebrum, a name phonetically and linguistically related to the ancestor of the Hebrews, Eber, referred to in Genesis 10:21.

(c) Pettinato claimed initially that some of the names contained the theophoric element -ya, which he related to the divine name of the Hebrew god, Yahweh (also abbreviated -ya).

(d) In another text, Pettinato claimed (initially) that reference was made to five cities: Sodom, Gomorrah, Admah, Zeboiim, and Zoar. These are the same cities that are listed as the "cities of the plain" in Genesis 14. Other "biblical cities" were also mentioned, such as Jerusalem, Megiddo, and Ashdod.

Some details of the background may clarify the potential significance of claims such as these that Pettinato was making soon after the discovery. First, it is worth noting that according to the biblical record Abraham was associated with the ancient city of Haran, which geographically is located in the general vicinity of Ebla. Abraham, of course, probably lived several centuries after the Golden Age of Ebla; if we may assume that he was a real historical figure, he should be dated *circa* 1800 B.C. But the coincidence of Eblaite names with biblical names, and the coincidence of biblical Eber with Eblaite Ebrum, suggested that the civilization of Ebla was that from which the Hebrew culture may have emerged.

Second, the kind of evidence that Pettinato claimed to have found was particularly noteworthy in the context of biblical scholarship in the 1970s. A distinguished Canadian scholar, John Van Seters, had published a book in 1975 (which had been completed prior to the discovery) entitled *Abraham in History and*

Tradition. The book is a thoroughly academic work, with a sophisticated and complex argument. Its overall implication was to undermine the historical authenticity of the Abraham narratives in the book of Genesis, thus running contrary to the principal trend of American scholarship during the last several decades. Van Seters' book was simply symptomatic of a major debate that was emerging in biblical scholarship in the 1970s, quite independent of the excavations at Tell Mardikh. That debate focused on the historicity, or otherwise, of the patriarchal narratives in Genesis. And the chance discovery of ancient Ebla was seen by some scholars, and by even more who were not scholars, as a fortuitous (or providential) new set of data that could be utilized in settling the debate. At first glance, the rediscovery of Ebla appeared to swing the power in the debate back towards those who sought an essentially historical interpretation of Genesis 12 – 50.

But the issues are far from clear. What are we to make of the rediscovery of ancient Ebla? What is its relevance and significance to the study of Ugarit and of the Old Testament? It is best to begin any assessment with considerable caution. Between 1975 and 1980 there have been extraordinary claims made about the significance of the Ebla tablets and their relevance for the Bible. Most of these claims have been made by people who have never seen the tablets, who are unable to read the script or translate the languages, and who have never set foot in Syria. If Pettinato may be forgiven for what may have been rash claims, made in the excitement of discovery, some of his successors are not so quickly forgiven. (One Australian "scholar" even published a paperback book, using the "instant publishing" method, claiming essentially that Ebla has provided, finally, the absolute proof that the Bible is "true.") Against this rash of unsubstantiated claims, it should be pointed out that the first collection of Eblaite texts (G. Pettinato, *Testi Amministrativi della Biblioteca* [Naples]) was published (in Italian) in 1980, and thus has only just become available for careful "public" examination. It will take at least twenty years to publish the entire corpus of texts from Ebla, and that may be too optimistic a prediction. In other words, with respect to the matter of the precise contacts between the world of the Bible and Ugarit, and that of ancient Ebla, it will be many years yet before firm statements can be made. Common sense would indicate, then, that we face a long wait before the Ebla texts are sufficiently well known to be applied in detail to the understanding of the ancient Near Eastern world. There is a need for caution.

From this initial statement of caution, a further negative remark follows naturally. It is simply a mistake to jump onto the bandwagon that flies a banner "Ebla proves the Bible," and it is a mistake for two reasons. First, to make claims concerning the truth of a certain document on the basis of particular evidence that has not been seen and has not been carefully studied is dangerous; it is suicidal from an academic perspective and irresponsible from a theological or religious perspective. But second, it is a misguided enterprise in the first place; it is one part of a trend that is sweeping the current Christian world, that lays hold of any scrap of apparent evidence to support the "faith," whether it be the planks of Noah's ark, the tablets of Ebla, or the shroud of Turin. The movement is rooted in a loss of faith, which seeks to bolster its crumbling walls by laying hold of what are said to be "facts" supporting the veracity of the Bible after all these centuries. And from there, it quickly becomes a new kind of propaganda, designed to indicate the truth of religion. (And, almost without an obituary, "faith" dies in this whole process.) The irony of this contemporary trend in certain forms of religion is that, even if its proponents could establish what they claim, they would not have achieved their goal. To prove that the historical narrative of the Old Testament is accurate, if such were possible, does not prove the essential truth of the Bible — namely, what it says about God. That must always remain both the subject and the object of faith.

Yet, for all these negative and cautionary remarks, it would be foolish to go too far to the other extreme. Every scrap of information retrieved from Ebla helps to fill in our knowledge of the history and civilization of ancient Syria and the Middle East. And that knowledge in turn is a part of the context in which one must study both ancient Ugarit and the Old Testament.

2. The Discoveries at Ras Ibn Hani

Ras Ibn Hani is the name given to a promontory, about 4.3 miles north of downtown Latakia, and about 2.5 miles southwest of the bay, Minet el-Beida, adjacent to Ras Shamra. The promontory extends for about 1.5 miles westwards into the ocean, forming bays on both its northern and southern flanks. At some point in the past, the tip of the promontory was almost certainly an island;

the constant movements of the ocean eventually changed the topography to form the present situation.

It had been known for a long time, by both scholars and local residents, that there had been periods of habitation at Ras Ibn Hani in the distant past. René Dussaud, in a book published in 1927, had made reference to "Christian structures" (i.e., from Roman or later times) in the area. More significantly, Gabriel Saadé, in the first volume of his *History of Latakia* (1964), had indicated the presence of a number of small tells on the promontory and pointed to their potential significance. And then, in 1973, a funerary vault of Ugaritic type had been discovered in the northwestern section of the principal tell noted by Saadé.

Evidence of this kind made it clear that it would be worthwhile undertaking excavations at Ras Ibn Hani. The necessity of fairly hasty excavations had become clear by mid-1974. The promontory of Ras Ibn Hani was gradually being encroached upon by the suburban growth of the city of Latakia. Furthermore, plans had been made to build a large international resort hotel on the promontory itself. A dedication stone was positioned and a ceremony conducted, attended by President Hafez al-Assad, to mark the beginning of work on the hotel. But as the ground began to be

FIGURE 16: **Ras Ibn Hani, Syria**

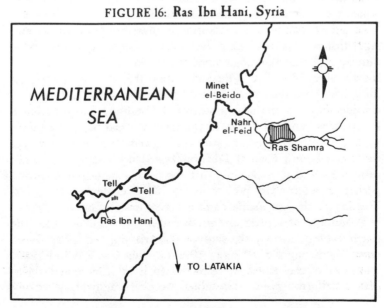

cleared for construction purposes, remains of ancient structures were found just below the topsoil.

Hence, a "salvage mission" was planned. The location of the hotel was moved a little to the south, away from the area where excavations would be conducted. A joint Syrian-French archaeological team was put together, with permission to undertake excavations over five seasons; Adnan Bounni, representing Syria, and Jacques Lagarce, representing France, were appointed co-directors of the excavations. On July 13, 1975, the site was surveyed; then the first archaeological campaign was conducted from July 16 to August 31, 1975. Further excavations were undertaken during the following summers.

The excavations at Ras Ibn Hani revealed, at different levels, that there had been various periods of settlement in the past. (1) On the main tell, evidence was found of a Byzantine settlement during the fourth to sixth centuries A.D. (2) Beneath that, evidence (notably, a variety of ceramic objects) indicated a period of Hellenistic settlement during the third to first centuries B.C. (3) A third level of occupation, dating from the eighth to sixth centuries, was characteristic of the Iron Age. (4) Finally, at the lowest level so far excavated, extensive evidence was found of a Late Bronze Age settlement, contemporary with the period in which the kingdom of Ugarit flourished.

It is the fourth level of excavation, representing the Late Bronze Age, that is of particular significance for the study of Ugarit. A number of large buildings were found that had been destroyed shortly after 1200 B.C., the same time that the city of Ugarit itself had been destroyed. One of these buildings had been of considerable size; the proportions of the building and its massive foundations indicated that in all probability it had been a "summer palace," constructed by the king of Ugarit. But it is clear that there had been a town at Ras Ibn Hani, not merely a summer residence. And it is possible that the town had begun to grow, perhaps as a secondary port to that at Minet el-Beida, prior to its invasion by the Sea Peoples and eventual destruction.

A number of aspects of this discovery are significant for the larger context, namely the study of Ugarit and the Bible. First, especially during the 1977 and 1978 campaigns at Ras Ibn Hani, a number of clay tablets were found, in both syllabic and alphabetic cuneiform writing. The tablets were all fragmentary, having been broken when the buildings in which they were stored collapsed, centuries in the past. They were also diverse as to character, including economic texts, administrative letters, ritual texts, and mythological texts. While the texts themselves are interesting and important, it is what they indicate that is even more significant; if the town at Ras Ibn Hani were typical of a small town in the kingdom of Ugarit, then all the other small towns (hidden in tells yet to be excavated) may also hold further collections of texts awaiting discovery. The discovery of Ugaritic texts in various small towns outside the capital city will be of enormous assistance in coming to a fuller understanding of what life was like in the ancient kingdom of Ugarit.

The second feature of particular interest at Ras Ibn Hani pertains to the evidence of resettlement at the site, immediately after its destruction. Apparently the Sea Peoples, who destroyed the town, rebuilt part of it and continued to live there. (There is no clear evidence of similar reoccupation at Ras Shamra/Ugarit.) The structures giving evidence of the resettlement are far less impressive than the original buildings, being somewhat cruder. But they provide real physical evidence of some small part of the culture of those barbarian people who created such havoc on the entire eastern coast of the Mediterranean Sea during the twelfth century B.C. Prior to the discoveries at Ras Ibn Hani, there has been very little in the way of physical evidence of the culture of the Sea Peoples.

To summarize, the discoveries at Tell Mardikh and Ras Ibn Hani, while highly significant as such, are nevertheless symptomatic of the treasures that remain to be found. Ebla fills in the historical background to Ugarit and the civilization of ancient Syria; Ras Ibn Hani demonstrates that after fifty years a vast amount remains to be discovered about the civilization of Ugarit as such. And all these discoveries, and the potential of the future, may contribute bit by bit to our knowledge of the ancient world in which the biblical narrative is set.

A knowledge of Ugarit is important in its own right; it is a part of the patchwork of past civilization which is being patiently reconstructed, a past from which our own civilization is partially derived. And it is also important in providing a knowledge of the ancient world that will enable a more informed reading of the text of the Bible.

Chapter VII:
A GUIDE FOR
FURTHER STUDY
AND READING

THIS final chapter, a postscript, contains a series of notes and comments that are intended to be of assistance to those who desire to study the subject matter in more detail. First, there are some comments on the site, museums, and general bibliography; then, the paragraphs that follow provide notes and more detailed reading with respect to the subject matter of each of the main chapters of this book (Chapters II through VI).

1. Ras Shamra: The Site

The site is located only a few miles north of Latakia, Syria's principal seaport on the Mediterranean coast. It is a short and inexpensive taxi ride to the site itself from the city. There is usually a guardian/guide on duty at the site who can be of considerable assistance (unless one is fortunate enough to visit the site while an excavation is in process). The physical extent of the excavations, after more than half a century since the rediscovery, is enormous, and it is wise to allow a few hours for walking on and around the entire tell to absorb the atmosphere of the place. Some postcards and reproductions (of a cuneiform alphabet) are usually available at the site. (The weary traveler may discover the excellent restaurant, only a short distance from the tell, where the waiters are experienced excavators!)

To make a full day of it, it is worth visiting Ras Ibn Hani on the return trip to Latakia. Indeed, with the new resort hotel operational, it would make an excellent base. The Ras Ibn Hani excavations are literally on the back doorstep, on the central and northern portion of the promontory. Both the hotel and the excavations are at the northern extremity of the city of Latakia, in a beautiful coastal location.

2. Museum Collections

There is a small museum in the town of Latakia, but its holdings are extremely limited. The principal museums to visit are those in Damascus, Aleppo, and Paris.

The Louvre in Paris contains many of the artifacts and texts discovered at Ras Shamra during the excavations prior to the Second World War, during which period Alawiya (now a part of the Syrian Arab Republic) was a French protectorate. In the main section of the museum (Salle XVIII), there is a fine display of artifacts from both Ras Shamra and Minet el-Beida; stelae, ivory objects, tools (inscribed), and other items of interest may be seen. The clay tablets held by the Louvre are not displayed in the main museum, but are held in the administrative section, the Conservatory. (Note: the artifacts recovered during the excavations undertaken between 1929 and 1939 were divided into two collections, one deposited in the Louvre, the other in the museum at Aleppo.)

The National Museum of Damascus and the National Museum of Aleppo both have excellent exhibits of their various collections of Ras Shamra materials. Objects recovered in the excavations from 1948 to 1965 were deposited in Damascus; since 1966, new discoveries have been deposited in Aleppo, adding to the items that were placed there prior to the Second World War. It should be noted that all objects now discovered are required by law to remain in Syria; this law has been in effect since the Second World War.

The only tablets held in North America are the so-called "Claremont Tablets." These were purchased in France on behalf of the Institute for Antiquity and Christianity, Claremont, California.

3. Bibliographies

An enormous body of literature, both of primary and of secondary studies, has accumulated on the subject of Ras Shamra/Ugarit during the period of more than fifty years since the rediscovery of the ancient city. The basic bibliographical guide is a massive four-volume work: Kurt Bergerhof, Manfried Dietrich, and Oswald Loretz, *Ugaritische Bibliographie der Jahre 1928-1966* (Neukirchen-Vluyn: Neukirchener). Volume 1 covers 1928-1950; volume 2 covers 1950-1959; volume 3 covers 1959-1966; the fourth and largest volume contains detailed indexes (by author, title, topic, etc.). More recent bibliographical coverage is contained in the *Newsletter for Ugaritic Studies*, published three times a year since 1972, with details of new discoveries, excavation reports, and detailed bibliographies of current research. Every ten issues of the *Newsletter* are reprinted (paperback), with the addition of indexes, to make them useful bibliographical guides: Peter C. Craigie, *Ugaritic Studies I: 1972-1976* (Calgary, Alberta: Canadian Society of Biblical Studies— Society of Biblical Literature, Section for Ugaritic Studies, 1976) and *II: 1976-1979* (1980). Guides to reading on particular topics can be found in the paragraphs that follow.

4. The Rediscovery of a Lost City: Notes on Chapter II

Claude F. A. Schaeffer's reports of the respective campaigns were published initially in the periodical *Syria*, beginning with his first report: "Les fouilles de Minet-el-Beida et de Ras Shamra," *Syria* 10 (1929): 285ff. More popular accounts were published in the *National Geographic Magazine*, 58 (1930) and 64 (1933), and in the *Illustrated London News*, beginning with no. 4724 (November 2, 1929).

Detailed studies of the decipherment of the Ugaritic script can be found in the following three articles: Charles Virolleaud, "Le déchiffrement des tablettes alphabétiques de Ras Shamra," *Syria* 12 (1931): 15-23; Hans Bauer, "Die Entzifferung des Keilschriftalphabets von Ras Shamra," *Forschungen und Fortschritte* 6 (1930): 306-7 (this was the study received by Virolleaud in August 1930); Édouard Dhorme, "Un nouvel alphabet sémitique," *Revue Biblique* 39 (1930): 571-77. More popular accounts may be found in Leo Deuel, *The Treasures of Time* (Cleveland: World, 1961); Maurice Pope, *The Story of Decipherment: from Egyptian Hieroglyphic to Linear B* (London: Thames and Hudson, 1975); and David Kahn, *The Code Breakers: The Story of Secret Writing* (New York: Macmillan, 1967).

The most comprehensive study of Ras Shamra/Ugarit, covering the first ten years of excavation, is provided in Robert de Langhe's two-volume work, *Les textes de Ras Shamra-Ugarit et leurs rapports avec le milieu biblique de l'Ancien Testament* (Paris: Desclée de Brouwer, 1945). Perhaps the most useful general survey of all the excavations, the nature of the discoveries, and the civilization of Ugarit is to be found in Gabriel Saadé, *Ougarit: Métropole Cananéenne* (Beirut: Imprimerie Catholique, 1979).

5. Life in Ancient Ugarit: Notes on Chapter III

The history of Ugarit is recounted in Mario Liverani, *Storia di Ugarit: nell'età degli archivi politici* (Rome: Centro di Studi Semitici, 1962). The general history of the period may be found in William F. Albright, *The Amarna Letters from Palestine, Syria, the Philistines, and Phoenicia*, the *Cambridge Ancient History*, 3rd ed. (New York) 2 (1973): 98-116, 507-536. On the end of Ugarit's history, see Michael C. Astour, "New Evidence of the Last Days of Ugarit," *American Journal of Archaeology* 69 (1965): 253-58. A useful general account of the state of Ugarit has been written by Anson F. Rainey, "The Kingdom of Ugarit," pp. 76-99 in Edward F. Campbell, Jr., and David N. Freedman, eds., *The Biblical Archaeologist Reader* 3 (Garden City: Doubleday, 1970).

The following studies provide more detailed information concerning various aspects of life and society in ancient Ugarit: H. Frost, "The Stone Anchors of Ugarit," *Ugaritica* 4 (1957): 235-245; Michael Heltzer, "The Metal Trade of Ugarit and the Problem of Transportation of Commercial Goods," *Iraq* 39 (1977): 203-211; *The Rural Community in Ancient Ugarit* (Wiesbaden: Reichert, 1976); E. Lipiński, "An Ugaritic Letter to Amenophis III Concerning Trade with Alašiya," *Iraq* 39 (1977): 213-17; Dennis Pardee, "The Ugaritic Text 2106: 10-18: A Bottomry Loan?" *Journal of the American Oriental Society* 95 (1975): 612-19; Anson F. Rainey, "The Military Personnel of Ugarit," *Journal of Near Eastern Studies* 24 (1965): 17-27. On Ugaritic religion, see André Caquot and Maurice Sznycer, *Ugaritic Religion* (Leiden: Brill, 1980).

6. Ugaritic Language and Literature: Notes on Chapter IV

The most useful introductory handbook to Ugaritic studies is Cyrus H. Gordon's *Ugaritic Textbook*. Analecta Orientalia 38 (Rome:

Pontifical Biblical Institute, 1965). This marvellous work contains the principal Ugaritic texts in transliteration, a selection of texts reproduced in alphabetic cuneiform, a glossary of the Ugaritic language, and a concise grammar of Ugaritic, including comments on the nature of Ugaritic literature.

The tablets were published in a variety of different books and journals following their initial discovery. There are two principal editions of the texts. The first is a two-volume work by Andrée Herdner, *Corpus des Tablettes en Cunéiformes Alphabétiques* (Paris: Imprimerie Nationale, 1963); these two volumes contain the texts discovered between 1929 and 1939. The first of the two volumes contains the texts in transliteration, with notes and bibliographies; the second volume contains both hand copies of the cuneiform texts together with photographic plates. The more up-to-date and comprehensive edition of the texts is that of Manfried Dietrich, Oswald Loretz, and J. Sanmartín, *Die keilalphabetischen Texte aus Ugarit* (Neukirchen-Vluyn: Neukirchener, 1976); this volume contains all the texts found prior to 1976, in transliteration only.

A number of guides are useful in the study of Ugaritic texts. For the study of words, there is an invaluable concordance: Richard E. Whitaker, *A Concordance of the Ugaritic Literature* (Cambridge, Massachusetts: Harvard, 1972). There is also a "concordance" to the different numbering systems that have been used to designate the texts: Manfried Dietrich and Oswald Loretz, *Konkordanz der ugaritischen Textzählung* (Neukirchen-Vluyn: Neukirchener, 1972). And apart from the glossary found in Gordon's *Ugaritic Textbook* (above), an Ugaritic-German glossary is available: Joseph Aistleitner, *Wörterbuch der ugaritischen Sprache*, 4th ed. (Berlin: Akademie, 1974).

Several translations are available, in which the literary Ugaritic texts are rendered into modern languages. Michael D. Coogan has produced a very readable translation of the principal mythological and literary texts: *Stories from Ancient Canaan* (Philadelphia: Westminster, 1978). A broad cross-section of texts in English is provided in Cyrus H. Gordon, *Ugaritic Literature* (Rome: Pontifical Biblical Institute, 1949). The most indispensable book for students is J.C.L. Gibson's *Canaanite Myths and Legends*, 2nd ed. (Edinburgh: Clark, 1978); this work contains the Ugaritic texts set out on the left-hand page, with the English translation on the facing page. It also has a very useful Ugaritic-English glossary. The most valuable French translation of the texts is by André Caquot, Maurice Sznycer, and Andrée Herdner, *Textes Ougaritiques 1: Mythes et Légendes* (Paris: Éditions du Cerf, 1974). In addition to these translations of several Ugaritic texts, a number of monographs have appeared containing a translation and detailed study of various single texts. One of the most useful of such volumes is John Gray's *The KRT Text in the Literature of Ras Shamra*, 2nd ed. (Leiden: Brill, 1964).

7. The Old Testament and Ugaritic Studies: Notes on Chapter V

A number of introductions and general studies of the relationship between Ugarit and the Old Testament have been published. There are two useful introductions, though both are now slightly dated: Arvid S. Kapelrud, *The Ras Shamra Discoveries and the Old Testament* (Oxford: Blackwell, 1963) and Charles F. Pfeiffer, *Ras Shamra and the Bible* (Grand Rapids: Baker, 1962). A similar volume is available in French: Edmond Jacob, *Ras Shamra-Ugarit et l'Ancien Testament* (Neuchâtel: Delachaux et Niestlé, 1960). A volume which covers some of the same ground but is a pioneering and original work in its own right is John Gray's *The Legacy of Canaan: The Ras Shamra Texts and their Relevance to the Old Testament*, 2nd ed. Supplements to Vetus Testamentum 5 (Leiden: Brill, 1965). For a survey of comparative studies on Ugarit and the Old Testament, see Peter C. Craigie, "Ugarit and the Bible," pp. 99-111 in Gordon D. Young, ed., *Ugarit in Retrospect* (Winona Lake: Eisenbrauns, 1981). The more detailed notes that follow provide further reading for the series of examples of comparative studies provided in Chapter V.

(a) *Psalm 29*. Harold L. Ginsberg, "A Phoenician Hymn in the Psalter," pp. 472-76 in *XIX Congresso Internazionale degli Orientalisti* (Rome: 1935). Theodor H. Gaster, "Psalm 29," *Jewish Quarterly Review* 37 (1946-1947): 55-65. Frank M. Cross, Jr., "Notes on a Canaanite Psalm in the Old Testament," *Bulletin of the American Schools of Oriental Research* 117 (1950): 19-21. F. Charles Fensham, "Psalm 29 and Ugarit," pp. 84-99 in *Studies On the Psalms* (Potchefstroom, South Africa: Ou Testamentiese Werkgemeenskap, 1963). Peter C. Craigie, "Psalm

XXIX in the Hebrew Poetic Tradition," *Vetus Testamentum* 22 (1972): 143-151; "Parallel Word Pairs in Ugaritic Poetry: A Critical Evaluation of their Relevance for Psalm 29," *Ugarit-Forschungen* 11 (1979): 135-140.

(b) *Amos the "Shepherd."* Scandinavian scholars who have proposed sacral connotations to the term *nqd* include Ivan Engnell, *Studies in Divine Kingship in the Ancient Near East*, 2nd ed. (Oxford: Blackwell, 1967) and Erling Hammershaimb, *The Book of Amos* (Oxford: Blackwell, 1970). For a broader perspective on the Ugaritic evidence and its relevance to the Old Testament term *nqd*, see B. Cutler and J. MacDonald, "The Unique Ugaritic Text UT 113 and the Question of 'Guilds,' " *Ugarit-Forschungen* 9 (1977): 13-30, and Peter C. Craigie, "Amos the *nōqēd* in the light of Ugaritic," *Studies in Religion/Sciences Religieuses* 11 (1982): 29-33.

(c) *On Cooking a Kid.* For background information, see the following: Charles Virolleaud, "La naissance des dieux gracieux et beaux: Poème phénicien de Ras Shamra," *Syria* 14 (1933): 128-151; Harold L. Ginsberg, "Notes on 'The Birth of the Gracious and Beautiful Gods,' " *Journal of the Royal Asiatic Society* (1935), pp. 45-72; Peter C. Craigie, "Deuteronomy and Ugaritic Studies," *Tyndale Bulletin* 28 (1977): 155-169.

(d) *Psalm 104*. The general background to the subject may be found in James H. Breasted, *The Dawn of Conscience* (1933; reprinted, New York: Scribner's, 1968), p. 368, and Eric W. Heaton, *Solomon's New Men* (New York: Pica, 1975). For detailed studies of the topic, see Georges Nagel, "À propos des rapports du Psaume 104 avec les textes égyptians," pp. 395-403 in Walter Baumgartner et al., eds., *Festschrift Alfred Bertholet* (Tübingen: Mohr, 1950), and Peter C. Craigie, "The Comparison of Hebrew Poetry: Psalm 104 in the Light of Egyptian and Ugaritic Poetry," *Semitics* 4 (1974): 10-21.

(e) *The Musical Background to the Psalms*. The stereo recording of ancient Hurrian music from Ugarit is by Anne D. Kilmer, Richard L. Crocker, and Robert R. Brown, "Sounds from Silence: Recent Discoveries in Ancient Near Eastern Music" (a booklet and twelve-inch stereo record; Berkeley: Bīt Enki, 1977). The original edition of the tablet was published by Emmanuel Laroche, *Ugaritica* 5 (1968): 463-64. On the implication of the recording for the Psalms, see the introduction in Peter C. Craigie, *The Book of Psalms* 1 (Waco: Word, 1982).

(f) *Hurrians, Hebrews, and Covenant.* The proposal concerning the interpretation of the Hurrian text is presented in Peter C. Craigie, "EL.BRT.EL.DN (RS.24.278, 14-15)," *Ugarit-Forschungen* 5 (1973): 278-79. For further analysis, see Kenneth A. Kitchen, "Egypt, Ugarit, Qatna and Covenant," *Ugarit-Forschungen* 11 (1979): 453-464. On the Egyptian background to the word "covenant," see Craigie, *The Book of Deuteronomy.* New International Commentary on the Old Testament (Grand Rapids: Eerdmans, 1976), pp. 79-83.

(g) *"Ships" in Judges 5.* The initial suggestion was made by John Gray, *Joshua, Judges and Ruth* (London: Nelson, 1967), pp. 287-88. Additional textual evidence is provided in Peter C. Craigie, "Three Ugaritic Notes on the Song of Deborah," *Journal for the Study of the Old Testament* 2 (1976): 33-49.

(h) *Ugarit, Israel, and the Greeks.* On the relationship between Ugaritic and Greek civilization, see T. B. L. Webster, *From Mycenae to Homer* (New York: Norton, 1964), and P. Walcot, "The Comparative Study of Ugaritic and Greek Literature," *Ugarit-Forschungen* 1 (1969): 111-18; 2 (1970): 273-75; 4 (1972): 129-133. On the possible Greek antecedents to Isaiah 14, see J. W. McKay, "Helel and the Dawn-Goddess," *Vetus Testamentum* 20 (1970): 451-464. On the Ugaritic background to Isaiah 14, see Peter C. Craigie, "Helel, Athtar and Phaethon (Jes 14 12-15)," *Zeitschrift für die alttestamentliche Wissenschaft* 85 (1973): 223-25.

(i) *Baal and the Exodus.* For a fuller analysis of the Ugaritic-Canaanite background to the Song of the Sea, see Frank M. Cross, Jr., "The Song of the Sea and Canaanite Myth," *Journal for Theology and the Church* 5 (1968): 1-25, and Peter C. Craigie, "The Poetry of Ugarit and Israel," *Tyndale Bulletin* 22 (1971): 19-26.

8. New Discoveries: Notes on Chapter VI

(a) *Ebla.* The story of Ebla's rediscovery is told clearly in Chaim Bermont and Michael Weitzman, *Ebla: A Revelation in Archaeology* (New York: Times Books, 1979). For further studies of the implications of Ebla with respect to Ugarit and the Old Testament, see the following studies from an already voluminous bibliography: Giovanni Pettinato, "Ebla and the Bible," *Biblical Archaeology Review* 6/6 (1980): 38-41; Mitchell Dahood, "Ebla discoveries and biblical research," *The Month* 13 (1980): 275-281; "Eblaite, Ugaritic, and Hebrew Lexical Notes," *Ugarit-Forschungen* 11 (1979): 141-46; R. Althann, "The Impact of Ebla on Biblical Studies," *Religion in Southern Africa* 2/1 (1981): 39-47; Peter C. Craigie, "The Bible and Archaeology," *Chelsea Journal* 3/4 (1977): 261-63. More detailed bibliographical references may be found in the *Newsletter for Ugaritic Studies* (see section 3, above).

(b) *Ras Ibn Hani.* The initial excavation reports were published by Adnan Bounni, Elisabeth and Jacques Lagarce, and Nassib Saliby, "Rapport préliminaire sur la première campagne de fouilles (1975) à Ibn Hani (Syrie)," *Syria* 53 (1976): 233-279, and "Rapport préliminaire sur la deuxième campagne de fouilles (1976) à Ibn Hani (Syrie)," *Syria* 55 (1978): 233-311.

Some preliminary and provisional studies of the texts from Ras Ibn Hani have also appeared: Andre Caquot, in *L'Annuaire du Collège de France* 79 (1977-1978), has provided translations and notes on some of the texts discovered in 1977 and in volume 80 (1978-1979) on some discovered in 1978.